Lifestyle by Design
Step #1: Leveraging Expertise

Lifestyle by Design:

An 8-Step Guide to Building Wealth for

HOW TO MAKE MONEY, CHANGE YOUR MINDSET, CREATE HABITS FOR SUCCESS, and MANAGE WEALTH

Iresh Parker

Lifestyle by Design Step #1: Leveraging Expertise

Lifestyle by Design Step #1: Leveraging Expertise

*"You don't need money to make money! Think about it. If you had $100,000,000 stuffed under your mattress, you still wouldn't be making money. **ACTION** is what you need to make money! Without **ACTION**, you just have a lumpy mattress!"*

— Anonymous

Lifestyle by Design Step #1: Leveraging Expertise

Contents

Introduction

"You don't need to have any specialized knowledge. You just need to know where to find the right answers!"

Oh, another one of those books. It's alright; I would be thinking that, too.

What I am going to tell you is that this book isn't for most people. If you don't desire to improve your life, or if what you have is fine or enough, please don't buy it. I don't want you to! It won't work for you and *that* doesn't work for me. Only 10% of people are ready to believe they can have more. Of those 10%, only 5% will strive through the actions in this book and improve. So, if you desire better, more, and are willing to take action, buy the book. Or don't, and know that you are off the hook because it wouldn't work for you anyway.

This book series is not magic. It is not a "get 'rich' quick" scam and it will not do anything for you just by purchasing it. Before deciding to purchase this book, you must be able to analyze your readiness and answer these questions:

- What do you want to get out of purchasing this book?

- How do you see this book helping you?

- What strengths do you already have that will contribute to your success?

- Can you commit an hour a day to reading this book?

- Can you commit 2 or 3 hours per week to taking action?

- How will you schedule or manage your time differently so that you can achieve success?

- Are you willing and able to dedicate time, effort, and energy to reading this book and achieving your dreams?

This book and the entire series will provide knowledge and tools for your success. It is up to you to hold a burning ambition, learn, and act.

This book is part of the *Lifestyle by Design: An 8-Step Guide to Building Wealth* series. This series includes *Step #1: Leveraging Expertise*, *Step #2: Deal or No Deal*, *Step #3: Wholesaling*, *Step #4: Rehabs*, *Step #5 Lease Options*, *Step #6: Flip 2 Rent*, *Step #7:Systemize & Prioritize*, and *Step #8: SUCCESS*. The books *Step #1*, *Step #2*, *Step #7*, and *Step #8* are must-reads!

The books *Step #3, Step #4*, *Step #5* and *Step #6* involve choosing your own adventure, which means you can choose one, many, or all! The two supplemental guidebooks, *Secret Real Estate Niche* and *Sold*, are written in support of—and guidance through—your personalized adventure, created by your choices in books *Step #3* through *Step #6*. All of these elements, when taken together, will generate a synergistic power, allowing you to design your life instead of just living it!

Since we all live in the real world and life seems to keep getting in the way of our trying to get things done, at the bare minimum, you *need*—and we all know *need* really means *should,* since mind control is not yet an option—to read and complete the **Ready, Aim, Fire** section of each chapter (otherwise, you will be Ready, Fire, Aim). The **Ready, Aim, Fire** section was engineered to counterbalance all of the excuses such as "I don't have time and I already know most of that anyway, so I don't really have to read it," and "I'll just skip ahead and come back to it later." I can hear my motivational coach now; those are all insignificant and irritating fear manifestations and should be squished flat.

The **Ready** section is a brief summation, with high points and key factors, of the entire chapter. Even if you read the whole chapter, please read the **Ready** section. As a reward for reading the entire chapter, you only have to read it once. To all others—skimmers, speed readers, and skippers—read the **Ready** section twice! The sense of the book can only be marginally interactive. The best choice for learning and retaining information is for me to tell you what I'm going to teach you, teach you, and then tell you what I just taught you. Thus, we have the creation of the brief summation of the **Ready** section.

The **Aim** section is both a guide and a journey calculated to construct a mindset excursion, specific to each chapter. It is a frame of reference to create a state of consciousness and cognitive function, distinct to each chapter's subject, allowing you to visualize and empower the fundamental lessons. The idea behind the **Aim** section is to use the power behind The Law of Attraction, The Universal Consciousness, The Power of Positive Thinking, or whatever you would like to call it, to create a prophecy demanding to be fulfilled, and for you to take action! Aiming is about precision, focus, and determination. It is directed. It is also the unswerving drive fueling the action of your **Fire**!

The **Fire** section is check-boxed, bullet-pointed perfection. Other than the **Aim** section of each and every chapter, it is the most profound and the most powerful section. The obscure, crazy scientist, Albert Einstein, is credited for stating that the definition of insanity is doing the same thing over and over again and expecting a different result. **Nothing in your life will change without action!** Let me say that again. **NOTHING IN YOUR LIFE WILL CHANGE WITHOUT ACTION!** The **Fire** section is where you take action and is where you get your money's worth. This is where 90% of you will be left in the dust. That's right, the difference between success and failure. It is the difference between designing your life and living it! Meticulously checkmark every checkbox after the task is complete. Conscientiously follow and complete each bullet-pointed list. What else can I say? Let me use Nike's slogan: "Just Do It!"

Many of the **Aim** and **Fire** exercises in this book and in this series capitalize on the concept of reverse engineering. In a nutshell, I worked backwards so you can work forwards. Please try it my way. If, however, it doesn't work for you, please feel free to reorder my reverse engineering. Remember that action is more important than perfection! Doing what works, even if it is a variation on my suggestions, is more important than doing everything just as suggested. Results matter, not any slight deviations you take to accomplish them!

Timeout (*author creates a T with hands*). I can hear you asking, "Is this 'action thing' really that important?" Yes! The entire book series is devised to push you to take action. Only when we are pushed, prodded, shoved, forced, driven, launched, and propelled outside of our comfort zones can we grow. If you are not happy with your current lifestyle, if you want something better either for yourself or for someone else, or if you are reading this book, something inside of you wishes and yearns to grow. My job as your provisional exhibitor through the chaos is to cajole, coax, and entice you to take, at the very least, a single step outside of your comfort zone, towards growth. My hope is for all of my readers to take several; however, I *know* that less than 15% of you will take just one. Please, prove me wrong. I dare you!

Time in (*author creates a T with hands*). Due diligence is extremely important. As your advisor and model during your adventure, I am going to tell you little bit about me. Don't worry, I'll keep it short. I am an active real estate investor.

My goal in writing this series is to conquer the fears of the select few who are willing to change their actions and expectations, allowing them to design their lifestyle. Because the balance of wealth in this country is unfair, I grappled with composing a way to reach the greatest number of people, allowing for both the greatest degree of change and the best use of my time to give back. Inspiration struck and this book series practically wrote itself, driven by my passion and desire to get the word out to as many potential world-changing individuals as possible.

Lifestyle by Design Step #1: Leveraging Expertise

Chapter 1: Steps to Goal-Setting

"The only thing standing between you and your goal is the bullshit story you keep telling yourself as to why you can't achieve it." – Jordan Belfort, Wolf of Wall Street

I can already hear you saying, "Not this again!" I know, I know. Every motivational, inspirational, self-help, business, or productivity book contains at least one chapter—most of them several chapters—on setting, tracking, and achieving goals and the importance thereof. There exist shelves, probably even stores, of books containing information about everything you ever wanted to know, and everything you *never* wanted to know, about goals. Endeavoring not to waste anyone's time, and in an attempt to remain from being trite, we're only going to review goals concisely. Goals are important because:

1) They help you achieve success.
2) They make the intangible tangible.
3) They build SYNERGY, by increasing confidence and establish the **Habit of Success**.

How many bad habits do we all have? Millions, right? How difficult is it to break bad habits? Super hard, right? Now, imagine all of that bad habit negative momentum working for you instead of against you, giving you the potential to have SUCCESS as the worst of all of your bad habits! By correctly and actively using goals, success—both personal and professional—becomes a habit! Wow, wouldn't that be wonderful?

Setting goals is not about achieving them. Believe it or not, it's not even about changing yourself into the person who can pull off those goals. Goals are way more important than most people realize. Their hidden purpose is to create a resilient clarity of consciousness and combine them with focus of intentions and empower your ability to achieve whatever is sought. The principal is to inspire lucid visualization. Visualization, the creation of images to communicate, is the simplest, most powerful, and oldest way to communicate both abstract and concrete ideas.

Visualization has existed since the dawn of humanity—cave drawings (as per Dr. Angela Kessell, Stanford University and Barbara Tversky, Columbia Teachers College, in their 2008 research paper *Cognitive Methods for Visualizing Space, Time, and Agents)*. Goals are the lighthouse on the shore of the stormiest, most violent, churning, and chaotic seas of your life!

Imagine the most complicated, convoluted, and complex maze. Now mirror the maze and place the original maze and the mirrored maze side-by-side. Then, take the new, side-by-side image and mirror that. Then place the new, side-by-side image and the mirror of the side-by-side image side-by-side. Are you confused yet? You get it, it's complicated. Into that convoluted mess of the visual image, insert stepping stones that clearly indicate the exact path needed to transverse from beginning to end and complete your maze successfully. By stepping stones, I mean goals.

In order to reach the point of creating and setting goals, we need an ending in mind. By simply starting the process of thinking about goals, the first steps of capitalizing on the most powerful form of communication—Visualization—has already been achieved.

The fog starts to clear, the sea begins to calm, and the sun winks to life on the horizon. True Visualization is gained when we clearly picture ourselves within and/or receiving the outcome of our vision.

To help us do this, we need to concentrate on mastering our mindsets. How important is your mindset? Paramount! Your mindset determines the overall success that you have in all areas of your life. Your mindset affects each and every aspect of your life. A mistake many investors make is only focusing on the mechanics of their strategies and not the psychology behind the mechanics. What you do and how you do it starts and ends with your mindset. How do you react to failures? How you react to successes? These things matter in determining your success and how you carry yourself in the long run. Mindset is a simple idea that can make all the difference. It's important to understand mindset and how it works. Many people aren't aware of their own thoughts. Simple awareness is required to begin to really transform your success. As Stanford University psychology professor Carol S. Dweck pointed out, "the key isn't ability; it's whether you look at ability is something inherent that needs to be demonstrated, or something that can be developed." (This quote was taken from Michael E. Gerber, Than Merrill, and Paul Esajian's 2015 book, *The E Myth Real Estate Investor: Why Most Real Estate Investment Businesses Don't Work and What to Do About It.*)

Your mindset is simply your beliefs about yourself and your most basic qualities. Your intelligence, talent, and overall personality are all part of your mindset. Individuals process thoughts differently. Some people have more negative thoughts than positive thoughts, and vice versa. Modern expert psychologists believe that your mindset springs from a complex mix of nature and nurture. With experience, training, and overall personal effort, anything is possible for anyone.

There are 2 basic mindsets: the growth mindset and the fixed mindset. "In a growth mindset, people believe that their most basic abilities can be developed through dedication and hard work—brains and talent are just starting point. This view creates a love of learning and a resilience that is essential for great accomplishments," says Dr. Dweck, in her 2007 book, *Mindset: The New Psychology of Success*.

The key characteristics exhibited by individuals with a growth mindset are:
- ✓ Believes that intelligence can be developed
- ✓ Embraces challenges
- ✓ Has persistence in the face of setbacks
- ✓ Sees effort as a path to Lifestyle by Design
- ✓ Learns from criticism, constructive or otherwise
- ✓ Finds inspiration in the success of others
- ✓ Reaches higher levels of achievement
- ✓ Has a greater free will

It is important to develop and maintain a growth mindset. It will allow you to learn more and more quickly. You must believe that you have the ability to influence your life. If you do not, then how will you ever change it for the better? Only with a growth mindset can a person's true potential be known. With a growth mindset, it becomes impossible to predict an ending to an individual's accomplishment potential with years of passion, dedication, and education.

People who have a fixed mindset believe that intelligence and talent are genetic. If a person believes that talent is fixed and that it has everything to do with being successful, then effort takes no role at all. Unfortunately, most people tend to believe that they are either born intelligent or not, and are either qualified for a job or not. There's no growth potential involved. People with this mindset tend to look for someone to blame and point fingers. A fixed mindset won't allow an individual to grow and learn from their mistakes.

The key characteristics exhibited by individuals with a fixed mindset are:
- ✓ Believes in static, genetically determined intelligence
- ✓ Avoids challenges
- ✓ Gives up easily
- ✓ Sees effort as useless or worse
- ✓ Ignores constructive criticism
- ✓ Feels threatened by the success of others
- ✓ Plateaus early and achieves less than their full potential

The mindset you have today was created, altered, and cemented throughout your periods of development as a child. Gaining self-awareness is required before development can begin. A child who is told that they are good or not good at specific activities creates a fixed mindset.

Remember, both encouragement and criticism are necessary for growth. A fixed mindset is self-reinforcing; once its pattern is developed, it will very seldom go away without conscience, concerted effort. However, even if you feel you have a fixed mindset, there are ways to alter your interactions so that you can gain a growth mindset.

In order to reach our fullest potential, each person must begin to think differently. One must believe they are not chained to their current capabilities, that abilities are shaped and built as we grow. With this alteration to your mindset and awareness, growth becomes designing your lifestyle. The first steps are to be aware of ignorance, how we process thoughts, and what we say to others. Knowledge leads to solving the problem as we begin to embrace challenges and love learning, ensuring success. It is possible to have a fixed mindset and still have a growth mindset about specific things. It's also possible to have a growth mindset and a fixed mindset about one thing or another.

After developing an awareness of thoughts and how we communicate with others, an awareness must be developed of feelings. Changing feelings requires us to question ourselves with better questions. Modeling the success of others is one of the greatest skills anyone can learn. It allows people to experience the growth they are looking to develop. It can, if viewed with a growth mindset, push us to operate at a higher level.

I remember when I played volleyball in college. Our team was the top-ranked team in our conference; we were 11 and 0. When we played against the lowest-ranked team in our conference, there were two possible outcomes; unfortunately, we didn't believe we could lose. There is a difference between playing to win and playing not to lose, which I learned that day. The lowest-ranked conference team came to win. They were energized, focused, and had nothing to lose. They left everything on the court. We felt overconfident and destined to win. Consequently, we started making mistakes we would've never made against a better opponent because we didn't believe we needed to be at the top of our game. By facing off across the court with the best, the lowest-ranked team was able to exceed our momentary potential, not settle, strive for more, and reach the top of their game.

Most often, an individual with a fixed mindset avoids taking on new challenges because they fear failure. This keeps them from learning and growing. When we apply a growth mindset to business management, we learn that rejection isn't personal, nor is it a true door slammed in our face—even if it is. Rejection is a sign, pointing us in a new direction, and teaches us that criticism isn't an insult but a gift, helping us to overcome, improve, and grow. In business, we have to learn to accept it when others tell us no, as well as their criticisms and our failures. When we do, we are one step closer to improvement and a growth mindset!

Communication is a key indicator and one of the most important opportunities for us to develop growth mindsets. When communicating with others, our goal should be to make the people around us feel good about themselves while letting them know that we expect more from them, both in our personal and professional relationships. Telling someone that they are the best helps in creating a fixed mindset since you are unknowingly setting a fixed limit on their abilities—in essence, preventing them from becoming even better. A compliment about their hard work, dedication, or how far they have come creates a growth mindset by not setting a limit on their potential. These differences are minor; however, they make a big difference as we interact with people every day. By choosing our interactions with care, we are choosing our thoughts with care, and developing our growth mindset while helping others develop theirs.

Goal-setting is one of the best ways to practice and apply a growth mindset to both your personal and professional mindset. By setting goals, we can create an unconscious map to success. Knowing where you have come from, where you are today, coupled with setting goals, we decide where we want to be in the future. This change of perspective allows us to really focus on where we are going and how we are going to get there. Designating a step-by-step process and creating a system for goals and our future will allow us to design our lifestyle, live the life we want, and live our life by design.

Mastering visualization and envisioning your rewards is the first step to setting goals. What is important with visualization is not reaching your goal although envisioning your goal's achievement is something that you should do; however, what is more important is visualizing your reward from achieving your goals. To demonstrate this with an example, let's take the goal of buying a new car. If you have a goal to make an extra $30,000 to buy a new car, imagine yourself holding the money for sure; however, the most powerful image to visualize would be yourself buying and driving your new car. What kind of car is it? What color? Where would you take it? The greatest power comes from the visualization of your reward. When you visualize, you must believe you have already achieved your goal. This means you are telling your brain that you already have it. To be effective, you must hold this belief and spend 5 to 10 minutes every day visualizing your rewards for achieving your goals.

The second step to goal-setting is to attach emotion to the reward you are visualizing. Emotion begins with motivation. Before thinking about setting goals, you need to think about motivation—what drives you, pushes you, forces you to overcome, and maximizes your determination. Here's a secret to help get your started: It is never about money, it's always about what money will buy or create for you. Some of these include:

        ✓ Freedoms
        ✓ Adventures
        ✓ More time to spend with family
        ✓ Financial freedom

- ✓ Vacations
- ✓ No more mortgage
- ✓ A new car

Of course, we can all say that all of these things are nice and we wouldn't mind any of them; however, you have to value some more than others. You have to discover your personal motivation. This is critical because creating a Lifestyle by Design, while fun and rewarding, is challenging. During the trials of frustration, you will need to fall back on your motivating force, also known as your Why. In the Fire section of this chapter is a series of questions that are designed to help you find your previously unknown motivations. These questions will help you create the intense, burning desire and energy to build your Lifestyle by Design—the life you have always wanted!

As with all things worth doing, developing a growth mindset, using goal-setting, and understanding that your motivation is all a process and a cycle, as is its inverse, demotivation. The first stage is belief, the second stage is potential, the third stage is action, and the fourth stage is success.

- ✓ BELIEF
- ✓ POTENTIAL
- ✓ ACTION

✓ SUCCESS

Our thoughts and beliefs create our ideas. You must **BELIEVE** that you have the potential. Think of your bedroom in your home. When you walk into the room at night and you can't see because it's dark, you reach out and flip on the light switch. You don't think about it, wonder if it might not work, or hesitate because you don't have the strength to flip the switch. You simply reach out and turn it on! As a matter of fact, you are surprised and disappointed if the light doesn't turn on or blows when you flip the switch. You have an expectation of **SUCCESS** from switching the light on and a firmly-rooted, subconscious **BELIEF** in the success of flipping the light switch and receiving the reward of light in the darkness. You need to develop this kind of belief in your own potential and success. The development of your belief in yourself will not happen overnight. It takes practice and failures before it can be achieved. Even when you get there, it's an ongoing process, just like the light bulb that occasionally burns out and needs to be changed. However, it is important to keep this level of belief in the back of your mind as your goal.

Once you understand the power of your **BELIEF** in yourself, you realize that you are not living up to your true **POTENTIAL**. Through belief comes the understanding not just that you could do something more but that you CAN do something more. Your **POTENTIAL** is unlimited (unless you create limits for it through your thoughts and ideas) and all of your **POTENTIAL** is just waiting to be unlocked!

POTENTIAL leads to **ACTION**. Taking action is the only way to avoid insanity! As I mentioned earlier, the definition of insanity is doing the same thing over and over again and expecting a different result. Without action, nothing ever changes. Without action, the results are always what you have had before and what you have right now. Because you are reading this book, on some level, you want change; you want more. Therefore, you must **TAKE ACTION!** Your action is the cause, the catalyst, the change, the power to design your life, to live by design, and your tool to achieve all of the rewards money can buy or get for you!

SUCCESS is the result of your taking **ACTION**, which is the result of your capitalizing on your **POTENTIAL**. It is also the manifestation of your **BELIEF** in yourself! **SUCCESS** breeds success. It creates a perpetual, reinforcing habit of more success. Achieving your goals and gaining your craved rewards strengthens your **MOTIVATION**, reinforces your **BELIEF**, increases your **POTENTIAL**, and leads to more **SUCCESS!** Creating a Lifestyle by Design will take time and effort; it won't happen in a day or a week. You need to remain motivated and disciplined. You can do this by making success your new habit!

Things to keep in mind as you are reaching for your Lifestyle by Design:

1. You don't need to be an expert to take action! You already have some foundations and specialized knowledge. You will acquire more from this book series. You will also learn about how to leverage the expertise of professionals, so let them be the experts while you grow and evolve.
2. Discipline will be both expected and necessary! Review your current workload and time commitments. You will have to schedule a specific time, every day, to work on your development and the creation of your designed lifestyle.

3. Quick and decisive implementation! Every time you learn something new that can help you, you need to help yourself grow by taking action **immediately! Every time!** Don't wait for tomorrow or the day after, or even the next day. It is too easy for tomorrow to become next month, next year, and then never! Be different, exceptional, and take action **NOW!**

4. Progression, not perfection! Done is better than perfect! Perfection is an unattainable goal and part of a fixed mindset, as it creates an absolute limit. People with a growth mindset know that perfection can be their worst enemy, as it is often used as a justification for fear. If you are waiting for the "perfect" time, it will **NEVER** come.

5. Learn from others instead of reinventing the wheel! The fastest way to build success is by duplicating what others have done that works. Learn from their mistakes instead of making them yourself. It's a shortcut. Read books on knowing your Why, goal-setting, negotiating win-wins, changing your mindset, etc. Make sure that you take advantage of all of the other people

out there that are massively successful. Listen to talks by internationally acclaimed motivational speakers and authors such as Les Brown, Tony Robbins, and Zig Ziglar, who said, "You will get all you want in life if you help enough other people get what they want."

6. Don't expect other people to understand and remember that it isn't your obligation to make them understand! The 1%-ers are called that because they constitute 1% of the income in this country, not the 99% of everyone else. If they were ready to consider the changes you are looking to make, they would have bought this book as well. Please keep in mind that I wrote this book because I don't believe that the wealth equation in this country is fair. However, I don't expect more than 5% of the people who read it to actually take action. If I only worried about the majority, I would neglect the 5% who will take action and be successful, rather than helping them.

7. Surround yourself with uplifting and positive people! At the very least, absolutely avoid negative people! You can't afford to let those people

hold you down and keep you locked into your old patterns. You need to surround yourself with people that motivate you and push you to succeed. This will create synergy, which will build as they motivate you, and you, in turn, motivate them. Don't forget that teacher and coach Gary Kent said, "You can't soar with the eagles if you are hanging with the turkeys." As you strive for success and your success becomes a habit, you will raise your standards in life and start demanding more life!

8. Expect more from life! When you associate with positive and like-minded people, you begin to think like them, speak like them, and act like them. Your standards, expectations, and beliefs of what you can achieve grow. Belief in what's possible, your potential, and your accomplishments improve. Thus, your life immediately changes. Many studies on massive success, including those of Nicholas Christakis and James Fowler, co-authors of the 2009 book, *Connected: The Surprising Power of Our Social Networks and How They Shape Our Lives*, have proven that your net worth is the average of the

people you spend the most time with, so make a special effort to surround yourself with the most successful people you want to emulate!

The Optimistic Realist is your new ideal. Goals need to be both optimistic and realistic. This is the Optimistic Realist. You need to set highly challenging goals, yet your goals still need to remain in the realm of what is truly possible. This possibility is so that your subconscious will believe you when you create your goals. Goal-setting ranges tend to run from extremely pessimistic, which involves setting no goals and reinforcing unsuccessful habits, to extremely optimistic, which involves setting goals that are too high and reinforcing more habits of failure rather than success. The biggest difference between the two is that the extreme pessimist expects failure while the extreme optimist often can't handle failure. Therefore, the ideal place in this range is where you can operate as an optimistic realist and achieve approximately 80% of your goals. This means setting optimistic goals that are realistic and attainable, thus creating habits of success and achievement. If you reach only 20% of the goals that you set or all of the goals you set, you create negative habits and contribute to a fixed mindset. You should always be failing on some level, at something, so that you can learn to deal with failure.

It's important to avoid setting unrealistic goals because it can become a negative self-fulfilling prophecy, reinforcing negative habits, thoughts, and behaviors in all aspects of your life. Let's take a fictitious— but all too common—example. Joan is currently working in a job where she makes approximately $40,000 per year and has been for the last 5 years. Joan sets a "building wealth" goal to make $1,000,000 her first year. This is an example of an unrealistic goal because she has developed the habit, pattern, and mindset of making $40,000 a year for the last 5 years. When she creates a goal to make $1,000,000 in a year, her subconscious rebels and doesn't believe in her or her goal. Unfortunately, her conscious mind is set on making $1,000,000. As the year goes by, and when the end of the year comes, she realizes that she isn't going to reach her goal of $1,000,000 and believes that goal-setting isn't working for her. Even when she makes $120,000, which is three times her annual salary, she still feels like a complete failure because she is so far from her goal. If she continues to set unrealistic goals, the negative belief of her feeling like a failure will persist and be reinforced. Eventually, she will believe that she is a failure who can't build wealth and it will begin to affect all areas of her life. She will begin to believe, both subconsciously and consciously, that she is a complete and total failure. This belief will affect her potential, her actions, and her results, impacting her personal and professional life, her relationships, and her dreams.

However, Joan is not a failure at all! She was actually very successful in her first year of goal-setting! The problem is that Joan just didn't have the skills needed to make $1,000,000, as she had only been making a salary of $40,000. Imagine if Joan was, instead, an optimistic realist and had set her first year's goal at $150,000. Achievement of so much of her goal and being so close to achieving it would have motivated her to strive and push forward, reinforcing her belief in goal-setting and herself. Her results would have shown her that her actions were starting to pay off. Joan would have pushed herself, been excited, and reinforced her belief in herself. She would have then set a goal for the following year of $275,000, followed by a goal of $500,000, and a 5-year goal of making $1,000,000. By using the reverse engineering method and creating smaller, realistic, stepping-stone goals, Joan could be comfortably making $1,000,000 per year by now. Joan's original goal, while not realistic for her, is actually very realistic for others. Yet, for most people, a goal of $120,000 is unrealistic. No one can determine what skills anyone else has, nor what a realistic goal is for anyone else. Each individual is in a different situation and at a different place in their life and development. The important takeaway is that each individual needs to emulate the optimistic realist and set both challenging and realistic goals.

How to Create and Set Your Goals

You might be new to wealth-building or be a seasoned veteran, focused on refinement rather than learning the system for the first time. Either way, designing your lifestyle and setting goals is not simply for your professional life. It is for your lifestyle, for every aspect of your life! This book is about discovering your personal Why and developing yourself, earning your ticket to the human race. The *Lifestyle by Design* series is about building and creating a better life for yourself and those you love. This system is not about overnight riches or getting rich quickly. It is about Wealth. If you stopped working actively today, how much you would need to live the life you want—your Lifestyle by Design—for the rest of your days? Whatever your number is—different for each and every one of us—is your ultimate, lifetime goal. Once your income is gathered and secured, you will have the freedom and choice to be able to design your lifestyle and start living it!

The main components of the *Lifestyle by Design* goal-setting and tracking systems are lifetime goals, annual goals, monthly goals, weekly goals, and daily goals. These goals should contain both personal and professional goals. Lifetime goals should be from 3-4 areas of your life and should contain 4-5 major aspirations for each of these areas. Remember to focus on rewards, which are never really money, rather than monetary goals. Then break these lifetime goals down into stepping-stone goals, as in what you need to achieve in the next 5 years, then 3 years, and then 1 year. When thinking about your lifetime goals, remember to consider your level of passion to complete the goal. Each lifetime goal should create a burning desire, a deep passion, and a limitless drive to accomplish it within your lifetime. Your emotions and feelings to accomplish your lifetime goals needs to motivate you to push yourself to succeed and strive to complete not only your annual goals but your monthly, weekly, and daily goals as well. They are the driving force behind your mindset, belief, potential, action, and success.

Your monthly goals are created from breaking down your annual goals, your weekly goals are created from breaking down your monthly goals, and your daily goals are created from breaking down your weekly goals. Each built from and reinforcing the other. These goals will build on your efforts to create a growth mindset as well as build and reinforce the habit of success.

At the beginning of your week, whichever day that is for you, set your weekly goals. Your weekly goals should then be broken down using the "Rule of 6" for your daily goals. This means you will break your weekly goals down to accomplish 6 things each day, which will help you reach 80% of your weekly goals, as the optimistic realist.

When creating your daily goals, use a time-setting method, as it will teach you how long completing tasks will take, allow you specific time periods—free of distractions—and allow you to keep track of your successes and failures over an entire year.

This will help you to both improve in the areas where you met obstacles and to celebrate your wins. Celebrating your successes and giving yourself rewards for accomplishing your goals is a critical step in reinforcing your positive, growth mindset. Every goal met at 80%, every success, every time you overcome an obstacle, and every time you improve by taking action **MUST** be celebrated! This is not optional. It is a requirement!

When creating your weekly goals, spend at least 10 minutes reviewing your monthly goals and your current year's annual goals. Use this opportunity to visualize the results and rewards of your annual and monthly goals, reinforce your motivation, belief, potential, and actions you will take. Look back at your goals for the previous weeks and/or months—if you have them—and fine-tune your upcoming week's goals to account for obstacles you faced so that you can accomplish even more. As you create these goals, remember that you want to focus visualizing your rewards/results, emotions, and motivations. Also, make sure they are SMART goals.

SMART
  ✓ **S**pecific—know exactly what you want

- ✓ **M**easureable—something you can quantify or count
- ✓ **A**ssignable—make sure you can and will hold yourself accountable
- ✓ **R**ealistic—you must **BELIEVE** that if you put in the work, you can and will achieve your goal
- ✓ **T**ime-Related—SMART goals have a measureable deadline

Making sure your goals are **SMART** is very important. In order to make sure your goals are **SMART**, you need to:

1. Keep your results and/or rewards in mind
2. Assign emotion to your achievement of those results
3. Use your visualization technique to fuel your motivation
4. Assign a specific amount of money you will need to generate to attain your rewards
5. Use the average income numbers from the income chapter, to break down your needed money to create measureable, hard numbers to generate the money you need
6. Now review each goal using the SMART methodology, answering these questions:
a. Is it specific?
b. Is it measureable?
c. Is it assignable? Are you solely responsible for the actions needed to achieve your own goals—not anyone else?

d. Is it realistic? Reach deep and be honest with yourself!
e. Is there a hard and fast deadline to hold you accountable?

Make sure you are creating weekly goals to include: income, via specific tasks assigned to generate a specific amount of money; education—including learning and reading from the *Lifestyle by Design: An 8-Step Guide to Building Wealth* series and implementing what you have learned; personal goals, including objectives to develop your growth mindset in your everyday communications, thoughts, and ideas; and healthy living goals, such as eating properly and exercising regularly. Personal goals are important to include because your personal relationships have a large impact on your effective time management and the time you spend on everything else. Also be sure to include healthy living goals because they have a direct impact on your energy level. The more energy you have, the more productive and the more successful you will become. Additionally, you should create a goal that pushes you, makes you really reach and flex your potential, and drives yourself forward!

While creating daily goals, spend 5 minutes at the beginning of each day putting your weekly goals into specific sets of distraction-free times. Make sure that, for the designated time period, you are focusing on a single goal, without distraction. Use your daily goals tracking worksheet to chart your progress. At the end of each day, spend 5 minutes transferring your progress on your daily goals tracking worksheet back to your weekly goal-tracking worksheet and calculate your overall progress.

Back near the beginning of the 20th century, an inventor and engineer named Nikola Tesla proved a very important concept that laid the foundation for immense and important discoveries and scientific advances. The 1st Law of Thermal Dynamics states that energy cannot be created nor destroyed, only transformed, and Tesla showed us that everything operates on a specific transmission or wavelength—everything in the universe! Therefore, if you want to achieve more, accomplish more, and succeed more while failing less, you need to transform and increase your vibration and frequency. In order to raise your vibration and frequency you need energy. The more energy you have, the more you can raise your vibration and frequency, attracting and generating even more success through focus, action, and determination. It all starts with energy and personal energy starts with healthy living.

I use the words "healthy living" instead of "fitness" because, even though most people believe that being healthy and fit are the same thing, in reality, they can be and are potentially separate states of being. A person can be very fit and not very healthy, and vice versa. Health, as defined by the World Health Organization (WHO) is a complete state of physical, mental, emotional, and social well-being—not merely the absence of disease or infirmity. It includes aging well, longevity, quality of life, freedom from pain, etc. Fitness is defined as a set of attributes that people have or develop as they relate to the ability to perform physical activity. Your goal should be a balance of both; however, health is necessary to achieve and develop fitness and is the first step to increasing your internal energy level, allowing you to raise your vibration and frequency, which will amplify your productivity and, eventually, your success!

READY?

The key takeaways from this chapter are:

- Goals are important because
  - They help you achieve success
  - The make the intangible tangible
  - The build synergy by creating the habit of success
- Visualization is the oldest and most powerful form of communication
  - Visualization allows you to channel the power of your subconscious into helping you achieve your goals
  - Remember to visualize the reward for achieving your goals and not just the accomplishment of your goals
- Create emotion to stimulate motivation
  - Remember it is never about money
  - It is about what money can buy for you and create for you:
    - ✓ Freedoms
    - ✓ Adventures
    - ✓ More time to spend with family

- ✓ Financial freedom
- ✓ Vacations
- ✓ No more mortgage
- ✓ A new car
- There is a pattern to motivation and demotivation
  - ○ Belief—remember the light switch
  - ○ Potential—whatever limit you set
  - ○ Action—required for change
  - ○ Results—the beginning and end of the cycle, reinforcing the pattern
- Develop and maintain a growth mindset
  - ○ A belief that intelligence and talent can be improved and developed
  - ○ Development of your mindset begins in childhood
  - ○ With conscious, concentrated effort, your mindset can be changed
  - ○ Surrounding yourself with positive, successful people will push your and drive you to grow
  - ○ Integrate your growth mindset into your day-to-day life, through your thoughts, ideas,

and the way you communicate with others
- Visualize your rewards and set goals to maximize your potential
- Remember, while reaching for your Lifestyle by Design:
  - You don't need to be an expert to take action
  - Discipline and dedication are both expected and necessary
  - Implement what you have learned quickly and decisively
  - Progression, not perfection, is needed
  - Learn from others rather than trying to reinvent the wheel
  - It is not your responsibility to make sure others understand
  - Surround yourself with uplifting and positive people
  - Expect more from life and yourself
- When setting your goals keep in mind:
  - The optimistic realist and 80% success
  - You should always be failing on some level so that you learn to handle setbacks
  - Everyone's skill sets and experiences are different

- o No one can write your goals for you
  - o Be honest with yourself
- Reverse-engineer your goals
  - o Start from your lifetime goals, as they drive and motivate all of your other goals
  - o Build annual goals from lifetime goals
  - o Build monthly goals from annual goals
  - o Build weekly goals from monthly goals
  - o Build daily goals from weekly goals
  - o Track all of your goal progress, both successes and failures
  - o When setting weekly goals, use the Rule of 6
  - o When creating daily goals, use set time periods
  - o Spend 10 minutes at the beginning of each week reviewing and visualizing the rewards of your lifetime, annual, and monthly goals
  - o Spend 5 minutes at the beginning of each day transferring your weekly goals into specific time periods of daily goals

- o Spend 5 minutes at the end of each day updating your daily and weekly goals worksheet
- Create SMART goals
  - o Specific
  - o Measurable
  - o Assignable
  - o Realistic
  - o Time-Related
- Energy, Vibration, and Frequency through healthy living

AIM.

In order to attach emotions and create motivations, understanding your reasons is critical! The AIM section will help you frame your thoughts and ideas, to capture your mindset, and stimulate and focus your thoughts to take action!

1. What are the most important things in your life and why?
2. What have you always wanted to do but haven't had the money to do?
3. What are the 3 best achievements in your life?
4. What are your 3 greatest strengths?
5. What day-to-day heroes exist in your life that you can take inspiration from?
6. What is your dream job? Why?
7. What is your financial dream? Why?
8. What is your health dream? Why?
9. If your time and wealth were unlimited, what would you do to give back? Why?

Imagine driving in the country with your wife, your daughter, her husband, and your granddaughter. Driving along the side of a river in the shade of forest trees, you travel for about an hour and finally arrive at a wrought iron, decorative gate, open on a long driveway that leads you closer to the river and deeper into the forest. Continuing up the driveway, you approach a beautiful, Victorian style château with a dark walnut door and inlaid with stained glass. The drive wraps around in a crescent and encapsulates a 12-foot water fountain feature made of marble.

The front door is ajar and you walk in with your family while your wife and your daughter ask you, "What's going on? Whose house is this?" Walking your family through the atrium in the entrance, into a fully-furnished living room, you ask everyone to take a seat.

Turning to your wife you say, "Honey, when you agreed to marry me, I made a promise that, one day, I would have enough to take care of not just us but our children and their children as well. Today is the manifestation of the success of that promise. Not only have I accumulated enough wealth for us, I have enough to take care of our daughter, her husband, and our granddaughter."

Turning to your granddaughter you hold out a set of keys and say, "Baby girl, these are the keys to this house and it's yours."

Visualize the pictures of the story you just read. Now read it again. What emotions do you feel when you picture it in your mind? What thoughts? Keep those feelings as you move on to the FIRE section.

FIRE!

TAKE ACTION! Without action, nothing will change. You will not grow or develop, goals will fail, dreams with wither, wealth will remain out of reach, and you won't be able to achieve your Lifestyle by Design. In fact, without action, you will NEVER be able to live your life by design.

Action steps to take NOW:

- Because I am committed to your success, the fundamental concepts in this chapter are so IMPORTANT and I want to celebrate your success in taking action to purchase this book, I want to give you a free reward. If you navigate to http://www.inspirationalbusiness.us and enter your name and email address, an email will be sent with a link to download your free daily goal creation and tracking worksheet.
- Get a journal, notebook, notepad, or something else to write on and a pen to write with. Answer the questions presented in this section. They will help you explore your deepest motivations. These answers are only for you! Be honest with yourself and

be as deep and as personal as possible.

Motivation Discovery and Building Action Steps

1. What do you do for your job?
2. Why do you do it? Don't overthink this one. Just write what comes to mind,
3. How does what you do contribute to making you a better person?
4. How does what you do contribute to making the world a better place?
5. What is your dream job? Why?
6. What ideals do you consistently argue for or against with others?
7. What beliefs does your stance indicate?
8. What makes you the angriest about the current state of the world?
9. Thinking about the next generation, whether or not you have children, what makes you most afraid?
10. Think about the 3 times you have been happiest in your life and write them down.
11. Choose the one where you were the most happy and write why you were so happy.
12. What excites you?
13. If you had limitless resources, what would you do to give back? Why?

14. Close your eyes and picture your ideal world. How is the world in your vision different from the current world?

15. Read and review your written answers to all of the above questions. Keep them in mind and write down 3-5 beliefs that you are most passionate about.

16. Does what you do, currently, allow you to accomplish and reinforce those beliefs? (If yes, describe how your work allows you to live your Why. If no, what can you do to combine your work with your Why?)

17. If your current work makes it impossible or even doesn't encourage you to live your Why, then list 3-5 possible jobs (hint: look at your answer to the question about your dream job) that would assist you in living your why and supporting your core beliefs.

Goal-Building and Goal-Setting Action Steps

1. Write down 3 of the best accomplishments in your life.

2. Write down your top 3 strengths.

3. Write down 5-10 different goal ideals.

4. From your goal ideals, create 3-5 different goals (hint: make sure they are SMART).

5. Choose at least one of your above goals (more is better) and list the tasks you would need to execute in order to accomplish that goal.

6. Put all of the tasks listed above into order.

7. Using your answers to the first and second questions, list what you did to help you reach one of your greatest accomplishments and what strengths you used to achieve it.

8. Write down 3-5 specific ways you will use the answers from your list in #7 and your strengths from #2 to help you accomplish at least one of your goals from #4.

9. Use your answer from the above motivational section and your Why to write down 3-4 areas of your life where you want to create massive and deeply emotional changes, aspects where you feel a burning desire to do something more.

10. Chose at least two of the areas you wrote down in #9 to create 3-5 aspirations for each area.

11. Using the 3-5 aspirations you just completed, create 3-5 5-year goals.

12. Using at least one of the 5-year goals you just wrote down, create 6 annual goals you need to achieve, as stepping-stone goals, in order to reach your 5-year goal.

13. Using at least one of the annual goals you just wrote down for the current year, create a stepping-stone goal for each month over the next 12 months to help you reach at least one of the goals for the current year.

14. Using the goal for the coming month that you just wrote down, practice creating stepping-stone goals for the next week. Write down, using the Rule of 6, your 6 goals for the coming week.

15. Using the 6 weekly goals you just created, practice creating a daily goal-tracking sheet with specific time period sets to accomplish one of the goals.

16. Evaluate your results. Right now, write this down for now and make sure you spend 5 minutes per day evaluating your daily, weekly, monthly, and yearly goals. (That's 5 minutes for each and every goal.)

Daily: What did I do right? What I can improve?

Weekly: What did I do right? What I can improve?

Monthly: What did I do right? What I can improve?

Yearly: What did I do right? What I can improve?

Now, take a break before you move on to Chapter 2, catch your mental breath, and **CELEBRATE** that you took action! **I really, really mean it! Stop and CELEBRATE!**

Chapter 2: Income and Hard Numbers

"Time is more valuable than money. You can get more money, but you cannot get more time." – Jim Rohn

There are three main types of income streams included in *Lifestyle by Design: An 8-Step Guide to Building Wealth:* Active, Investment, and Passive. The Active income stream is used to drive, generate, and create both the Investment and Passive income streams, while the Investment income stream is used to create only the Passive income stream. True wealth is calculated from the Passive income stream, which is the one used to design your lifestyle and live your life by design. We will look at these detail in this chapter.

Active income is the income you have to work for every day. It is the income that would stop accumulating immediately—or almost immediately—if you did nothing. It refers to income received from performing a service. This type of income includes wages, tips, salaries, commissions, and income from businesses in which there is material participation. For example, an accountant who works for a monthly paycheck receives active income.

For taxation purposes, the Internal Revenue Service (IRS) defines income as active if there is material participation by the individual or business.

To discern if income is active, consider these questions:
- Does the taxpayer perform the majority of the work?
- Does the taxpayer work 500 hours or more during the year to generate the income?
- If the taxpayer works less than 500 hours per year, are there any other staff members who work more hours than the taxpayer?

Active income, like anything else, has both pros and cons. One of the main advantages of active income is that earning active income typically carries a lower risk. For instance, an individual is participating in an activity to earn income, not risking capital in an attempt to earn passive income. Another advantage of earning active income is that it is predictable. Individuals generally receive the same monthly wage and know when it is going to be received, allowing them to plan and budget accordingly. For example, an employee who gets paid on the 15th of every month might allocate 30% of the received wage to mortgage repayments, 50% to other expenses, and 20% to discretionary expenses, such as saving for a vacation or going to restaurants. The main disadvantage of active income is that it can create limitations by encouraging a fixed mindset. Individuals who earn active income might become complacent, which could prevent them from discovering new opportunities. For example, an investment banker may be earning a lucrative salary and decide that it is not worth taking the risk to open his or her private hedge fund. Another disadvantage of earning active income is that it limits earnings potential. There are only so many hours in the day that an individual can work, which limits the amount of income that can be earned. For instance, a freelance writer who bills a client per article can only produce a limited amount of articles per day.

The financial definition (through professional emersion and years of experience in the financial market) for active income is slightly different from the IRS's. Financially, active income is defined as the regular compensation that an individual receives in the form of salary, wages, tips, commissions, and/or any other source of work. Rents, dividends, and interest payments are not considered active income because an individual does not need to do anything, other than invest, in order to earn them. An individual earns active income in order to pay for personal expenses, debt, and services. Active income, also called employment income, is the income necessary for an economy to function. Since this kind of income is necessary for an economy, and is the most common type of income, it is the income stream that the 99%-ers almost always earn and get stuck with earning, and the income that the 1%-ers are least likely to have and first to give up. In a very short timeframe—3-5 years for most people—it becomes completely unnecessary for building wealth and living by design!

Our next income stream is Investment income, also called Portfolio income. This kind of income comes from interest payments, dividends, capital gains collected upon the sale of securities or other assets, and any other profit made through an investment vehicle of any kind. Generally, individuals earn most of their total net income each year through regular employment income. However, disciplined saving and investment in the financial markets can grow moderate savings into large investment portfolios, yielding an investor a large annual investment income over time. Interest earned on bank accounts, dividends received from stock owned by mutual fund holdings, or sales of gold holdings would all be considered investment income. Income made on investments often undergoes different—and sometimes preferential—tax treatment, which varies from state to state, as per the IRS.

Businesses also can have income from investments. On their income statements, an item called "investment income or losses" is commonly listed. This is where the company reports the portion of the net income obtained through investments made with surplus cash, as opposed to being earned with the company's usual line of business. For a business, this may include all of the above, as well as interest earned or lost on its own bonds that have been issued, share buybacks, corporate spinoffs, dividends paid, and acquisitions.

Investment income refers solely to the financial gains above the original cost of the investment. The form the income takes, such as interest or dividend payments, is irrelevant to it being considered investment income as long as the income is generated from a previous investment. Additionally, investment income can be received as a lump sum or regular interest payments paid out over time.

In the simplest form, the interest accrued on a basic savings account is considered investment income. The interest is generated as an amount above and beyond the original investments, which are the deposits placed into the account, making it a source of income. Options, stocks, and bonds can also generate investment income. Whether this is through regular interest or dividend payments or selling a security at a higher rate than it was purchased, the funds above the original cost of the investment qualify as investment income.

Real estate transactions can also be considered investment income, and some investors choose to purchase real estate specifically as a way to generate investment income—in the form of capital gains experienced when selling property, deeds, notes, and/or interest payments for mortgages for Rehabbers. Once the original cost of the item is repaid, and payments received are not used for the purpose of covering other property-related expenses, the surplus income qualifies as investment income.

The majority of investment income has preferred taxation levels when the funds are withdrawn. For the most part, the tax rate is based on the form of investment which produced the income. Many retirement accounts, such as a 401(k) or a traditional IRA, are subject to taxation once the funds are withdrawn. Certain tax-favorable investments, such as a Roth IRA, are not taxed on eligible gains associated with a certain distributions as per the IRS.

An example of the unfair balance of wealth in this country is that the tax for the capital gains is 33%, while the current tax rate for withdrawing investment income is 37%. This means that investors who need to leverage their interest income to convert and build Passive income quickly, will pay twice as much. In an effort to keep them where they are, long-term capital gains and qualified long-term dividend income have a maximum of 20%, even if that amount exceeds a half-million dollars in a given year, per 2018 IRS tax codes. This means those who are already wealthy, who already have a fully-developed passive income stream, and are only developing their long-term investment or portfolio income streams get to keep more of their money and build their income faster!

"So, Iresh, you are telling us that we have to have money to make money and that the only way we can capitalize on the information in this book series is if we don't need it, right?" Absolutely not! I am telling you that you have to educate yourself, way more than someone who is already wealthy; you have to learn to work smarter and develop an entirely new set of skills and perspective to view the world.

Alright, so you don't want to pay 37% plus, potentially, another 33% and, potentially, a self-employment tax on top of all of that. I mean, really, who would be crazy enough to want to give away 75% of their investment income and capital gains? So, you need to leverage experts, as many as you can find. You need to go out and educate yourself! Start by learning about something often referred to as a Solo(k).

When you find a financial advisor, accountant, or an investment banker who knows what this is and can expand upon the knowledge I am about to give you, enlist their services, send them flowers, drive your kids across town to play with theirs, send your children to the same schools they send theirs, build rapport, and build an extensive relationship with them immediately! Why? Because they work with and cater their services to successful, wealthy individuals, who are exactly the kind of people you want to associate and surround yourself with.

A Solo(k), also known as a Self-Directed 401(k), is the best way to leverage your investment income to create, build, and generate your passive income! The first concept you need to understand is what a 401(k) is and how it works. A 401(k) is a qualified retirement plan that allows eligible employees of a company to save and invest for their own retirement on a tax-deferred basis. Only an employer is allowed to sponsor a 401(k) for their employees. The employee decides how much money they want deducted from their paycheck and deposit into their plan, based on limits imposed by their employer and the IRS rules. An employer may also choose to make contributions to the plan. Many of you who currently work for someone else probably have some kind of plan like this— either a 401(k) or, possibly, a 403(b). Additionally, employers have the responsibility to make sure that the plan is run in accordance with the laws, rules, regulations, and provisions of the plan and the government. This includes deciding who is eligible for the plan, how much the employer will contribute to the plan, what investment options employees will have, how often they can reallocate their investment assets, hiring the vendors necessary to run the plan, and what features the plan will have, i.e. will loans be allowed, if hardship withdrawals will be allowed, etc.

There are contribution limitations for tax deferrals, as determined by the Federal and State IRS. Since the state laws vary so much from state to state, you need to find an expert in your state. However, since the federal law is the same for all states, it is the foundation that I will discuss. Salary deferrals are $19,000 in 2019, plus an additional $6,000 in 2015-2019, if the employee is age 50 or older. What this means is that an employee can tax defer $19,000 per year into an investment account that they don't have to pay taxes on.

The next portion governed by the IRS is the annual compensation limit. In 2019, the annual compensation limit was $280,000. This is the place where most people don't understand and fail to maximize their savings. It has nothing to do with employee contributions, it has to do with employer matching funds. The gist is that your employer can only match funds with the employee until the employee reaches a YTD Gross income of $280,000. In an effort to clarify this concept, say you make $325,000. Sometime in November, your employer will have to stop matching your contributions. (An annual salary of $325,000 means, if you are paid monthly, you get paid approximately $350,000/12 = $27,083.33 per month. So, sometime in November, you will have reached the $280,000 mark, which means your annual compensation limit will be reached and the employer matching your contributions will stop.)

In order to maximize your employer matching funds, rather than the typical contribution schedule of ~$1,583.33 monthly contribution ($19,000/12 months), you would be better off contributing $1,900 monthly for the first 10 months. The reason is because, if your employer has a contribution matching plan at 50%, meaning they will match ½ of your contributions, following the second option, you will get your total annual contributions of $19,000 and your employer's maximum contribution for $9,500, for a total of $28,500 (excluding any catch-up allowances if you are 50 or older), rather than your $19,000 and your employer's $7,916.65, for a total of $26,916.65. I can hear you saying it's not that big of a difference, right? Now, imagine working for your employer for 10 years. It becomes a difference of $15,833.50. I don't know about you but I can say that the average person would be very pleased with an extra $15,833.50 over 10 years for no more effort than buying and reading two chapters in a single book.

The last restriction is regarding total employee and employer contributions. This must always be the lesser of 100% of an employee's compensation (and not the contributions), or $56,000 for 2019, and does not include any catch-up contributions for those age 50 and older. Taking our example from above, we know that an employee's contributions max out—for tax deferral purposes—at $19,000. So, what if a company, rather than matching 50%, matched 195% of employee contributions? Then, if you contributed your $1,900 per month to capitalize on your employer's annual compensation limit, your employer would contribute $3,705 per month in matching contributions. That means that the total annual contribution would be your $19,000 and your employer's matching contributions of $37,050—$37,000, actually, because of the $56,000 contribution limit. I can hear you asking, "But what employer would match their employees' contributions at 195%?"

Are you ready for a truly mind-blowing shift of perspective? In order to really leverage these concepts and capitalize on this potentially tax-saving opportunity, consider a new scenario, where you are both the employer and the employee. That's right. A person who is self-employed and is both the sole owner and sole employee of an S-Corporation receives a W2, just like any other employee—and this option nicely avoids paying any additional self-employment tax. As such, you are allowed to make contributions to a 401(k), just like any other employee, within the limitations and restrictions imposed by the IRS but, as the sole owner of the S-Corporation, you are also allowed to decide that the employer (also you) is going to match employee contributions at 195%. Let's take it one step further and integrate this concept with the concepts surrounding a Solo(k).

The financial difference, not the IRS difference, between a standard 401(k) and a Solo(k) is control. Control in and of itself is a very fluid and powerful concept, when leveraged correctly. As American businessman and politician Nelson Rockefeller said, "The secret to success is to own nothing, but control everything." A 401(k) is managed by a custodian and/or vendor and controlled by a trustee. Leveraging this idea and the secret of success, what if you controlled the trustee of your own 401(k)? Then you would control all of the assets that you contributed to your 401(k) account and their investment. This means that you, as the trustee, could invest your tax-deferred $56,000 annual income retirement account to build and generate your passive income stream! Yeah, awesome!

So, you, as the sole owner and sole employee of an S-Corporation, create a 401(k) account for your employee (also you) that is managed by one of a select few custodial companies which specialize in Solo(k) accounts and you, as the sole member and manager of an LLC—to capitalize on the long-term investment tax benefits—become the trustee of that Solo(k) account. That means, in effect, you have checkbook control of your 401(k) account contributions and can write checks to invest in whatever you want to create, build, and grow your passive income stream.

Since this chapter is all about income, let's postulate for a few minutes and see what we come up with. In certain, very profitable areas of the United States, an investor can buy a turn-key investment property for $80,000-$85,000 and make an income of $350-$400 profit per month per house, as per the National Association of Real Estate Investors 2018 Annual Report on the Real Estate Economy of the United States. Notice that I said "profit," which means after all costs and expenses. So, approximately, every year-and-a-half or so, from simply controlling your 401(k), you can purchase a turn-key property and begin generating a passive profit income of $350 per month and create a positive asset balance of $85,000.

For example, say you are 49 years old, looking to retire at the standard age of 67½, are self-employed, and have a Solo(k) account. In the 18½ years before your retirement, you could—as a way of avoiding taxes—purchase 12 turn-key properties and have a profitable, passive income of $4,200 per month. Additionally, remember that an S-Corporation may be the sole member of an LLC and you may be the solo employee of that S-Corporation and charge yourself a 90% fee for operating as the trustee of your Solo(k) account and controlling your investments. Now, your LLC can pay your second S-Corporation a fee of $3,780 per month for the profit of $4,200 per month generated from your passive income and control of your Solo(k) account. Then your second S-Corporation can generate a paycheck for you—unfortunately, you can only have one 401(k) contribution account per taxpayer number—of $3,500 per month—again avoiding the self-employment tax—and also avoiding any tax on distributions from your 401(k) tax-deferred account since fees are being paid and no distributions are being taken! Changing your perspective, therefore, means no 37% tax, no 33% capital gains tax, etc., and the ability to create, build, and design your own lifestyle!

At this point, a savvy investor starts including things like land trust agreements, leveraging multiple LLCs and S-Corporations for each of your investment types and assets. The example above is to open your eyes and mind to what is possible; to clue you into realizing that you didn't know what you didn't know; and to begin the process of creating a growth mindset, a perspective shift, and your educational potential. I am not an expert and I don't want you to do what I did at first! When my perspective suddenly expanded and my mind awakened to the possibilities, I went online as quickly as I could to figure out all of the possibilities available, to make myself an expert. Guess what happened? The next tax year, the IRS changed its mind and, instead of maximizing my money, I started shooting myself in the foot. I was no longer an expert—honestly, researching anything online, no matter how well you do it, really doesn't make you expert enough—and had to start all over. It was at this point that I learned the lesson of leveraging expertise.

Remember the tip I gave you about finding a financial advisor, accountant, or investment banker? Find one! Their job is to stay up-to-date on all of the tax laws and IRS changes, on both state and federal levels, so let them, and then leverage their expertise!

Maximize your time—remember, **TIME IS EVERYTHING**—and focus on making money for them to manage. Then, leverage their expertise to save more of the money you make!

Just remember to speak to the right kind of expert for the right questions. If you want to talk about the tax advantages, disadvantages, and not paying anymore to the government than you have to, talk to an accountant. If you want to make sure that everything you want to do is both legal and your best option to protect what you and/or your company controls, talk to an attorney. If you want to know about the best area of the United States to purchase turn-key properties, talk to a real estate investor that specializes in passive income development. Your job is not to know the answers to any of these questions. It is to have a general understanding of a given individual's expertise—or know where to find it—and to direct your questions to the right expert to make sure you are getting the right answers.

READY?

They key takeaways from this chapter are:

- There are three types of income streams included in *Lifestyle by Design: An 8-Step Guide to Building Wealth.*
- The first income stream is called the Active income stream and is typically generated by working, from salaries, wages, tips, etc.
- The second income stream is called the Investment or Portfolio income stream and is typically generated from capital gains of one kind or another.
- The third is the Passive income stream and is typically generated by doing nothing. It continues to come to you, without you needing to take any further action, for as long as you control whatever is generating the income.
- You need to shift your perspective and learn to look at the world through the eyes of the wealthy-minded individual.
- Learn to leverage expertise by getting a basic idea—or knowing where to find the basic idea—of any given expert's field of specialization

so that you can ask questions of the correct expert to make sure you get the right answers.

AIM.

In order to attach emotions and create motivations, understanding your reasons is critical! The AIM section will help you frame your thoughts and ideas, to capture your mindset, and stimulate and focus your thoughts to take action!

1. What are the three different types of income?
2. Which do you feel is the best for building wealth and your Lifestyle by Design?
3. Why?
4. Remember the example of maximizing 401(k) contributions. How can you incorporate them into your current situation?
5. What is the difference between a 401(k) and a Solo(k)?
6. What do you think Nelson Rockefeller meant when he said, "The secret to success is to own nothing, but control everything"?

FIRE!

TAKE ACTION! Without action, nothing will change. You will not grow or develop, goals will fail, dreams with wither, wealth will remain out of reach, and you won't be able to achieve your Lifestyle by Design. In fact, without action, you will **NEVER** be able to live your life by design.

- Get the same notebook, journal, or notepad, you used from the FIRE section of Chapter 1 and a writing utensil.
- Turn to a clean page.
- Write down your answers to the following questions:
  1. Using your favorite search engine—or even the telephone book—find 5 Certified Public Accountants in your local area.
  2. Write down their names and phone numbers/email addresses.
  3. Call all 5 of them and ask them about a Self-Directed 401(k). Say "I am enhancing my education and understanding of how to properly build wealth and I heard mention of something

called a Self-Directed 401(k). My mentor suggested that I contact a local CPA and get some more information. Do you have any information that you could share with me about Self-Directed 401(k)s?"

4. If they say yes and offer to send you information, give them your email address and read whatever they send you to make sure they understand what you are asking.

5. If they say yes and verbally give you information over the phone, you have your pen and paper ready to take notes and make sure they understand what you are asking.

6. If they say yes and ask to schedule an appointment to sit down and speak with you, thank them for their time. Let them know that you are in the early stages of gathering information and that you know their time is valuable. Ask if there is any general information they would be willing to send you or provide over the phone. Let them

know that you have a pen and paper ready. If they would still like to schedule an appointment, set one, and make sure you show up on time, with your pen and paper.

7. If they say no, thank them for their time and ask them whom they might recommend. Write down any information they provide and then move onto the next CPA.

8. If they all say no, call anyone else they recommended. If no one knows, then move on to the next 5 CPAs.

9. If no one in your local area can provide you with any information, move onto a larger area and begin calling another 5 CPAs in the larger area.

- Write down 3 ways that you can use the information you learned in this chapter in your current situation.

- If you can't think of any way to use it in your current situation, then write down 3 things that need to happen before you can use it and how you will use it then.

- Using the hard numbers listed in this chapter, $85,000 to purchase a turn-key property and a profit passive income of $350 per house, calculate what your Passive income requirements are to live your Lifestyle by Design.

- Wealth is the not the amount of money you have saved, or how many houses you own, or even the size of your business. Wealth is determined by your passive income. So, if you stopped working today, how many days would you have, living the same lifestyle you currently have, before your funds ran out? Write down your answer.
- Write down the balances in your retirement accounts. Add them up.
- Write down the balance in your business.
- Write down the balance in your personal bank accounts.
- Write down the balance of any additional accounts.
- Calculate your total available retirement funds and write it down.
- Write down your monthly expenses and calculate your total monthly expenses
- Multiply your total monthly expenses by 12 months and write down your total annual expenses.

- Write down your total monthly passive profit income.
- Multiply your total monthly passive profit income by 12 months and write down your total annual passive income.
- Now subtract your total annual expenses from your total annual passive income to calculate your total annual outflow.
- If your number is positive, what does this mean for the length of time you can sustain your lifestyle?
- If your number is negative, what does this mean for the length of time you can sustain your lifestyle?
- Now, divide your total available retirement funds by your total annual outflow (unless your number is positive). This number represents the total number of years you could maintain your current lifestyle if you stopped working today.
- Last, but not least, visualize your ideal lifestyle, your Lifestyle by Design. Calculate your monthly expenses and write them down. Divide that number by $350 and then add one, to calculate the number of houses you will need to control as passive income to maintain your Lifestyle by Design indefinitely. Write

down the total number of houses. Now, multiply that number by $85,000 and write it down. This is the total amount of money you will need to generate to reach your wealth and passive income goals.

- Spend the next 10 minutes thinking about other ways than the full amounts to purchase your number of houses. For example, putting down 20% to avoid PMI payments and mortgaging the balance of the home purchase or using a portfolio lender to multiple the total amount of money that you have available by a factor of at least 3. Could you, somehow, combine the two examples?

- After the 10 minutes, write down your ideas and work them into your total amount of money needed to purchase the number of houses your Lifestyle by Design will require.

Now, take a break before you move on to Chapter 3, catch your mental breath, and **CELEBRATE** that you took action! **I really, really mean it! Stop and CELEBRATE!**

Lifestyle by Design Step #1: Leveraging Expertise

Chapter 3: Business Entities and Asset Protection

"Why not invest your assets in the companies you really like? As Mae West said, 'Too much of a good thing can be wonderful.'" – Warren Buffett

When it comes to doing business, there are many different options available to choose from. The different options are to create a Sole Proprietorship or DBA, a Limited Liability Company or LLC, an S-Corporation, and a C-Corporation. Each option has its advantages and disadvantages as well as tax liabilities and tax compensations.

Each entity has its own process to create and maintain in order to actually capitalize on the benefits. At some time during your wealth-building journey, you will probably to have to create at least one of each and every one of them, except maybe a sole proprietorship, and probably more than one. Therefore, it would be beneficial to have, at the very least, a general understanding of each option.

What is a sole proprietorship and what are the advantages and disadvantages of starting a business as a sole proprietorship? Quite easily the most common business structure and the simplest out of all the other structures, a sole proprietorship is a business that is owned by only one person. Many people are confused whether the phrase applies to the business owned by one person or the one person who owns that business. It actually refers to both the business and the owner. In this type of structure, there is no legal distinction between the owner and the business.

To understand the concept further, let us break down the basic features of the sole proprietorship. A sole proprietorship is owned and run by one person, and that person often runs the business under his or her own name. A sole proprietorship does not have a separate legal entity. This is its major difference from partnerships and corporations. The sole proprietor (the owner) owns all the assets of the business. The sole proprietor also bears all the risks and the benefits associated with it. We can gain a better understanding of a sole proprietorship, and be aided in our decision on whether to choose this type of structure or not, by taking into account its various pros and cons.

A sole proprietorship is when the owner and the business are the same entity. This structure is the most simple and the easiest to understand. Forming a sole proprietorship is easy. Head to your local Secretary of State's office and file a single sheet of paper. When it comes to taxes, there is no differentiation between you and your business, so you are taxed as one. You are the business and run it however you want.

There are pros and cons to having a sole proprietorship, which are outlined in the following table:

The Pros	The Cons
Easy to dissolve if you change your mind—just pay all debts, close all accounts, and let the	Banks and lenders are reluctant to give loans due to higher turnover rates and usually smaller

tax man know	assets
You receive all business profits	Creditors and the courts go after personal assets such as your car, home, savings account, etc.
Smaller amounts of capital make for easier organization and less paperwork	Since the business relies on one person, it is fragile and can't be passed on easily

A limited liability corporation, better known as an LLC, is a business structure that combines pass-through taxation (like in a partnership or sole proprietorship) with the limited liability of a corporation.

An LLC is not a corporation—it is a legal form of a company that provides protection and limited liability to its owners. It's a combination of a corporation and a sole proprietorship.

There are pros and cons to having a limited liability corporation, which are outlined in the following table:

The Pros	The Cons
Flexible options for taxation, since you chose how you want to be taxed	LLC Members aren't paid wages
Less paperwork and filing costs than a corporation	High renewal fees or publication requirements depending on incorporation state
Can be a single member or an unlimited number of members	A few states have extra annual fees, either flat fees or a percentage based on revenue
Flow-through income taxation structure keeps things simple	Investors like bigger corporations better, occasionally making it harder to raise working capital
Members are protected from personal liability and the protection varies from state to state	Unless you're the sole member, you have less direct control over the business

Members can receive income/losses larger than their individual ownership percentage	

A corporation is a business entity that is legally separate from its owners. It has the right to enter into contracts, take legal action against others, give and receive loans, own assets, hire workers, and pay taxes. One of the most significant things about a corporation is its limited liability. That is, shareholders have the right to participate in the profits through stocks and paid dividends, but are not held personally accountable for the company's debts or legal issues that may arise.

A C-Corporation is a business entity that is taxed separately from its owners. Businesses are incorporated differently in all 50 states. All C-Corporations are required to issue financial statements.

An S-Corporation is a business entity that is federally taxed in a certain way. It is taxed as a pass-through entity by the IRS, just like a Sole Proprietorship or an LLC, which means no double taxation. An S-Corporation gives out stock and is treated much like a corporation. The owner or owners of an S-Corporation are called shareholders and they are protected from liability. There are a lot of advantages to S-Corporations, especially if you have a smaller or are just starting a business. An S-Corporation can also combine with an LLC.

There are pros and cons to having a corporation, which are outlined in the following table:

The Pros	The Cons
Owners are separate legal entities and not entirely responsible when faced with legal issues or debts	Time-consuming, expensive, and requires lots of paperwork
May sell stock to raise financial capital	Lots of regulations significantly decrees flexibility
Established structure, clear roles, accountability, and agendas	The corporation's profits and owner's dividends may be taxed, creating double taxation

Employees receive a W2 and are taxed as wage earners	Corporation is responsible to hold formal stockholder meetings and take notes

Since taxes, prices, and corporate laws are not the same in every state, one must consider a state's advantages and disadvantages when it comes to forming your business. Some things to consider when comparing states:

- Is it worth incorporating outside your home state?

- How are corporations taxed? What are the taxes?

- Would there be an income tax on my corporation?

- Is there a minimum or franchise tax?

- Compare projected revenue against cost of taxes to recognize any advantages.

- The best thing you can do is speak with an expert—like the CPA you found is the last chapter's **FIRE** section.

Iresh Parker

There is one additional entity which needs mentioning, a Trust. There are many different kinds of Trusts, used for a verity of functions; however, the basics are the same. A trust is created when an entity (guarantor) gives an asset (or assets) to an entity (trustee) to hold for the benefit an entity (beneficiary). The most common types of trusts are estate (Living) trusts and land trusts (we'll come back to land trusts later). Trusts are defined, for tax purposes, by the IRS, and you can speak with an accountant about their taxation classification coding; however, trusts are formed, regulated, and governed by both common and statutory law and you will need to speak with an attorney about their legal entity names and properties.

Estate trusts are typically broken down into two different types, a Revocable Living Trust and an Irrevocable Living Trust, as per the 2004 National Conference of Commissioners on Uniform State Laws. The difference between a Living Trust and a Will is that a Will is subject to probate, a court deciding ultimate distribution of assets. A Will can't provide creditor protection for the inheritance to your beneficiaries; a Will doesn't provide protection on government benefits for a person who is retired or disabled; a Will can't reduce Estate Taxes; a Will can't administer Assets to a minor without court intervention; and a Will isn't effective while you are still alive and, therefore, can't provide protection for your assets until you die, as per IRS and the Federal Internal Revenue Code (IRC). The difference between a Revocable and Irrevocable Living Trust is you retain control over your assets (Revocable) because the beneficiary of the estate (assets) doesn't change or you don't (Irrevocable) because it does.

Both your patience and attention are required. This next section is very important and an advanced concept. For maximum liability protection, tax benefits, and wealth-building, create two Trusts, an S-Corporation, two LLCs, and six bank accounts. Since an LLC can have any number of members, this also works if you have a business partner. The first LLC—the Working LLC—has the S-Corporation as its member and profit flows through the LLC to the S-Corporation. The shareholder of the S-Corporation is the first Trust—the Working Trust—and you are the employee of the S-Corporation and the trustee and beneficiary of this Trust. You will receive a W2 from the S-Corporation, as its employee. Since you are the Trustee of the Trust, you decide when and how to disburse dividend payments from the Trust, giving you the greatest flexibility, capitalizing on tax benefits. Additionally, as an employee, you can contribute to your own Solo(k) via your W2, taking advantage of both employer matching contributions and pre-tax deductions with the lowest chance of audit. The second LLC—the Holding LLC—has a member Trust—the second Trust created—the Holding Trust— of which you are also the Trustee and Beneficiary—and is used to manage the investments of your Solo(k) account. Each LLC, Trust, and the S-Corp will have separate bank accounts—with no SEC violations from co-mingling funds—and you will need a personal account, if you don't already have one, to deposit your paychecks into.

Let's walk through an example. Sam, a new real estate investor who purchased this book and is taking action, creates a "Working" LLC called Properties by Sam, LLC. Since LLCs have members rather than owners, Sam also creates an S-Corp called Managed Properties, Corp. Managed Properties, Corp is the member (owner) of Properties by Sam and Sam is the sole employee of Managed Properties, Corp. S-Corporations have shareholders rather than owners, so, protect himself, Sam doesn't want to be the owner of record for the S-Corporation. Sam contacts a local attorney and uses a broiler plate template, created by his local attorney, to create a "Working" Trust called Property Investments Trust. Property Investments Trust is the sole shareholder and owner of record for Managed Properties, Corp. To maintain control of his businesses and assets, Sam is both the Trustee and sole Beneficiary of Property Investments Trust and Managed Properties, Corp is the guarantor. Sam, as the Trustee of Property Investments Trust, instructs Managed Properties, Corp to create a 401(k) with employer contributions for all of its employees (Sam). Managed Properties, Corp then sets up an employee 401(k)—with one of the select few custodians that allow Solo(k) accounts—and creates a 401(k) account for Sam. Again, as the Trustee of Property Investments Trust, Sam works with the 401(k) custodian to create a "Holding" LLC called Investments by Sam and this LLC becomes the investment company for Sam's 401(k) funds. Investments by Sam, LLC also needs at least one member (owner), so Sam creates a "Holding" Trust called Managed Investments Trust of which Sam is the Trustee and Beneficiary and Investment by Sam, LLC is the guarantor.

Following the money through the above example, let's say Sam wants to purchase homes to rehab. Properties by Sam, LLC purchases 4 properties in a year. Then Properties by Sam, LLC sells the 4 houses for a profit of $50,000 per house, or $200,000 for the year. The profit from the house sales flows into the Properties by Sam, LLC bank account via a check from the title company. Properties by Sam, LLC then pays a distribution to its member, Managed Properties, Corp in the amount of 60% of its profits, or $120,000, which is paid via check from Properties by Sam, LLC's bank account and deposited into Managed Properties, Corp's bank account. Managed Properties, Corp generates a check for the 401(k), a paycheck for Sam, and a shareholder payment to Property Investments Trust. Because of the 401(k) account Sam created for himself, his contributions, and Managed Properties, Corp's employer contributions, $56,000 is paid to the custodian of the 401(k) account via a check from Managed Properties, Corp's bank account. The custodian of the

401(k) account then subtracts their management fees from the $56,000—usually 1.5% or as low as $500—and deposits the balance of the 401(k) contributions, $55,440, into the investment company, or Investments by Sam, LLC's bank account. Then Sam receives a direct deposit for his paycheck from Managed Properties, Corp into his personal bank account, $32,000, and a check from Managed Properties, Corp's bank account to Property Investments Trust's bank account, as a shareholder payment for $7,500. Except for Sam, as an employee, and Properties by Sam, LLC, all of the companies will show a loss—no taxes—and Sam will pay taxes on an income of the $32,000 annual salary, potentially capitalizing on things like the Working Childcare Tax Credit, Earned Income Credit, and Head of Household standard deductions. On paper, Sam made $32,000. But because he is in control of his Solo(k), he also has $55,440 in tax-free money he can leverage to create and build passive income.

Additionally, your S-Corp should be incorporated in Delaware—the best corporate protection state as this is the state where all of the Fortune 500 corporations incorporated according to the 2016 Annual issue of Fortune 500 Magazine. Your LLCs should be formed in two different states—ideally, the Working LLC in Nevada—the only Delaware of LLCs—and the Holding LLC in Oregon or Utah—as these are the states with corporate veil protection laws closest to Nevada—and your two Trusts should be formed in and governed by the laws of a third state—preferably South Dakota—the Delaware of trusts—and a fourth state, wherever you currently reside.

For clarity and cementation, let's look at an example. John's LLC owns three apartment complexes with 20 units each. John bought this book series, read it, took action, and leveraged professional experts. His S-Corporation is the member of the LLC and he is an employee of his S-Corporation. Additionally, each of his three complexes is held by a different Trust and every individual unit is also held by a different Trust. When a tenant in one of the apartments—Nathan—in one of the complexes—unit 1 of complex A—slips and falls inside his apartment, he decides to sue the owner for some easy money. Nathan retains an attorney to help him. Before an attorney decides to file a suit on his behalf, the attorney is going to do research to discover the assets of the owner. Using a property tax records search, he discovers that John's unit is held by a Trust and that the Trust only holds John's single unit. The attorney knows that he can't get very much money from a Trust holding a single unit and he needs to find out who runs the Trust and if it has any additional assets. Because Trusts are an agreement between parties, there is no way for Nathan's attorney to find out this information using public records. The attorney then goes to the local courthouse and files a motion to disclose the information about the Trust. John's attorney is also at the courthouse, responding to the motion, and agrees to provide the information on the Trust. However, he also reveals that the controlling party is an entity and was formed in the state of South Dakota (John's parent Trust). The judge then tells Nathan's attorney that he needs to file his motion in the state of South Dakota.

If Nathan has enough money, his attorney will file a motion in a South Dakota court. Again, John's attorney will appear and agree, only to reveal that the controller of the Trust is an entity and was formed in the state of Utah (John's holding company, an

LLC). The judge will then inform Nathan's attorney that he will need to file his motion in the state of Utah.

Again, if Nathan has enough money, his attorney will file a motion in a Utah court. This time, John's attorney will reveal that the controller is an entity that was formed in the state of Delaware (John's S-Corporation) and he will have to file a motion in the state of Delaware. By this time, if Nathan has enough money and hasn't given up, he should have purchased a home instead of renting an apartment and several investment properties as well, his attorney will move on to a Delaware court. At the very least, John, utilizing all of the time travel and the filing of these motions, created multiple additional entities, as many as needed since Trusts are free, and will wear Nathan's available funds into tatters, leaving all of John's assets fully-protected.

READY?

The key takeaways from this chapter are:

- The three main types of business entities are
  - Sole Proprietorships
  - LLCs
  - Corporations
- The pros and cons of each business entity revolve around differences between
  - Liability
  - Taxation
  - Control
- Requirements, taxes, and liability laws governing business entities vary by state
- Leverage the expertise of an accountant and an attorney when setting up your business and protecting your assets
- The two main types of Trusts are Estate Trusts and Land Trusts
  - The two main types of Estate Trusts are
    - Revocable Living Trusts—where assets remain in your control

- ▪ Irrevocable Living Trusts—where assets don't remain in your control
  - ○ Land Trusts are formed when one entity charges another entity to hold real estate or land in trust for a third entity
  - ○ Trusts are an agreement between parties and not a matter of public record
- Business entity creation and structuring is critical for asset protection
  - ○ If John, from the example, had owned all 3 complexes in his own name, then Nathan would have been able to sue for all of John's personal assets and income from all of the other properties as well.

AIM.

In order to create a business and protect your assets, understanding corporations and Trusts is critical! The AIM section will help you frame your thoughts and ideas, to capture your mindset, and stimulate and focus your thoughts to take action!

1. When you achieve your lifetime goals and start living your Lifestyle by Design, what kind of—and how many—assets will you have?

2. How will you protect those assets?

3. As you are building your wealth, what kinds of business will you set up?

4. How will you protect them?

5. What kind of structure does you current business—or the company you work for—have? Why?

6. Do you think it is the best one? Why?

7. How could you use a Trust to protect your current assets?

8. Would it be better for you to have a Living Trust or a Will? Why?

FIRE!

TAKE ACTION! Without action, nothing will change. You will not grow or develop, goals will fail, dreams with wither, wealth will remain out of reach, and you won't be able to achieve your Lifestyle by Design. In fact, without action, you will **NEVER** be able to live your life by design.

- Contact your local state bar and ask for an attorney that specializes in Land Trusts and an attorney that specializes in business start-ups.

- Contact the business attorney and let them know that you want to start a business and find out what information you need, as per your local laws.

  - You can find companies online that will perform incorporations, typically for less than a local attorney will. However, I would only suggest this option after meeting with a local attorney and getting a firm grasp of the annual requirements to keep your liability protection intact.

- o Make sure you are fully aware and fully prepared to meet all of these requirements yourself or purchase these services from the online company and/or the attorney. Otherwise, you will be throwing money away.

- Contact the attorney you were referred to for Trusts and ask them about creating a broiler plate or template for creating Trusts.

  - o Make sure that you tell them that a business will act as the Trustee and either you or a second business will be the beneficiary.

- Grab your notebook or journal and write down your top two

choices for potential business entities.

- Contact the accountant that you found in the last chapter. Ask the accountant about the tax advantages and disadvantages of your choices for potential business entities and write them down.

- Chose a business entity for your core business.

- Decide how you want to create your business entity, either online or with the help of a local attorney.

- Create your core business.

Now, take a break before you move on to Chapter 4, catch your mental breath, and **CELEBRATE** that you took action. Was it easier this time?

Chapter 4: Understanding the Wealth-Building Market

"Formula education will make you a living; self-education will make you a fortune." – John Rohn

This chapter will begin looking at the information you will need to know and where to find it. There are several terms you will need to understand while working your way through this series and when interacting with other professionals. These terms are constant and definitions will be forthcoming. Also provided are the processes and resources needed for independent local markets. Since this information varies from place to place, giving you the information for the areas I work in won't be helpful. Additionally, it won't teach you how to duplex the process across multiple different areas.

Don't worry; I will save the Glossary for last. (The underlined terms in this chapter can be found in the Glossary.) First, do we all agree that doing what works for the greatest number of other people has the greatest chance of working for you? If 100 people start picking fruit and 20 of them stop along the way and grab baskets and those 20 people bring back 5 times the fruit of everyone else, how many of the 100 people will stop to grab baskets on their way to pick fruit the next day? All 100, right? So, do what works! Agreed?

Keeping that concept in the front of your mind, understand that only 10% of the people in the United States have enough money to retire at age 65 and maintain a comfortable lifestyle until the average age of death at 80, 15 years later. In 2016, more than 300 economic experts recommended that the minimum retirement amount is one million dollars, according to the *Report of the National Commission for the Review of the Research and Development Programs of the United State Economic Community*. Every year since, both the cost of living and inflation has increased. By the time YOU are 65, who knows what the recommended minimum will be?

Less than 1% of the people able to retire comfortably at age 65 have enough to retire at age 50 or before. Of the 10% able to comfortably retire at age 65, 75% of them receive the majority of their retirement income as passive income from investing in real estate. Examining the 1% able to retire at 50 or before, 99% of them receive 83% or more of their passive income from real estate, according to the Bureau of Labor Statistics, Consumer Price Index for Urban Wage Earners and Clerical Workers and the 2010 Demographics Report by the United States Census Bureau. Now, are you ready to grab your basket before leaving to pick your fruit?

Rather than reinventing the wheel, a large part of this book series will detail everything you need to know, or where to find what you need to know, to get started investing in real estate. Obviously, the market we will be discussing is the real estate market.

In business and in real estate, your first understanding needs to come from a grasp of risks vs. rewards, the ROI (Return on Investment) potential, and the market divisions. The real estate market is divided into retail, commercial, and investor.

The retail market is comprised of mostly homeowners (and the occasional homeowner who owns a rental property or two) and 78% SFR (Single Family Residential) homes, according to the 2010 Demographics Report by the United States Census Bureau. The retail market is also known as the residential market.

The second division, the commercial market, is a mix of apartments, typically with more than 4 units—condos and true commercial properties, such as strip malls or office buildings. Most commercial properties are owned by businesses that are either involved with real estate, such as investors or Realtors, except for apartment complexes because they are mostly passed down through families. Most of the companies and other owners who own property in the commercial market do so for Buy and Hold—the Buy and Hold rental market consists of both short-term and long-term rentals—investing, typically to build passive income and hold the property long enough to avoid capital gains tax, instead of selling quickly or look to complete 1031 exchanges.

The Investor division is comprised of Flippers, Developers, and Lenders. The types of properties in order of increasing investor risk are Entry and Median SFR; Mobile Homes, Condos, Townhomes, and High-End SFR; Multi-Unit properties, Commercial properties, and vacant land. With vacant land having the highest risk, the least reward, and the lowest initial cost (unless purchased in very large quantities), it is typically the last arena in which investors work, according to the 2017 Annual Members Newsletter of the National Real Estate Investors Association. To find out where you should start, we need to level the real estate investor progress in terms of both time and investment capital.

1. Bird Dogs—for people with little time or capital
2. Wholesales—for people with tons of time and little capital, about $5,000 to $25,000 in working capital
3. Rehabs/Lease Options—for people with lots of time and a medium amount of capital, about $30,000 to $250,000 in working capital
4. Developments—for people with a medium amount of time and lots of capital, about $300,000 to $500,000 in working capital
5. Lenders—for people with little time and tons of capital, about $500,000 to $1,000,000 in working capital

6. <u>Turn-Key Buyers</u>—for people who have lots of consistent active and investment income and just need to build passive income and wealth. The time investment is little to none.

7. Lifestyle by Design

Where do you fit? Most people fit in spots 1, 2, or 3. It doesn't matter where you start, only that you DO start.

<u>Bird Dogs</u> focus on networking and interacting with <u>real estate investors</u>. It's a no-money-down strategy that can be lucrative for those with little time and little to no capital, who are willing to network and build relationships with investors. <u>Bird Dogs</u> potentially earn between $500 and $750 per referral, when the <u>real estate investor</u> creates a deal from their lead. They rely on a numbers game and the relationships they form with other investors to generate income. They market and sell their leads to <u>real estate investors</u>. A company that <u>Bird Dogs</u> so well that they have become <u>Wholesalers</u> is NetWorthRealty.

<u>Bird Dogs</u> start by understanding what their buyers want. All <u>real estate investors</u>, including <u>Buy and Hold</u> investors, want undervalued properties and distressed homeowners. Basically, they want the worst houses in good neighborhoods. <u>Bird Dogs</u>

need to cast the widest net possible to generate enough sellable leads to pay for their effort. Most real estate investors prefer buying properties without having to find a seller themselves, which is why they are interested in working with bird dogs. These real estate investors, on the other hand pay, the bird dog a finder's fee for a deal. Therefore, you can make money and practice finding deals, but only if you are self-motivated.

The largest real estate investment company in my area paid $62,618.93 to a single Bird Dog last year alone, for a total of 64 completed deals, some of which they bird-dogged to other investors, some of which they wholesaled, and some of which they rehabbed.

Wholesalers also focus on networking and relationships with investors. Wholesaling is more time-intensive than Bird Dogging because they assign contracts, sell options, sell beneficial interest, and sell deals. Wholesalers do the legwork that Bird Doggers don't. They actually put properties under contract—at least, they have an exclusive option to purchase contract and sometimes even purchase the property outright before selling it to another real estate investor. Because they put properties <u>under contract</u>, they are required to pay an <u>earnest money deposit</u>, usually 10% of the purchase price, to the property owner. <u>Wholesalers</u> also need to understand that <u>real estate investors</u> want undervalued properties and distressed homeowners. They, too, want the worst houses in good neighborhoods. Where <u>Bird Dogs</u> cast wide nets, <u>Wholesalers</u> need to specialize. They should choose a niche. Either focus on undervalued properties (Court <u>Probates</u>, <u>Tax Liens</u>, <u>Abatements</u>, etc.) or distressed owners (<u>Short Sales</u>, <u>Pre-Foreclosures</u>, <u>Underwater</u> Mortgages, etc.), even to the point of choosing a specific type within the undervalued properties or distressed properties. <u>Wholesalers</u> typically make between $3,000 and $5,000 per deal.

The same real estate investment company made $314,850 in Wholesales deals as the Seller and paid $54,392 in wholesale fees as the Buyer.

<u>Lease Optioners</u> operate in a category traditionally referred to as <u>Rent-to-Own</u>. They look for properties that don't need lots of repairs but mostly updates and light remodeling. <u>Lease Optioners</u> can provide the greatest benefit to homeowners that are in the earlier stages of hardship. However,

they can also benefit those in active foreclosure if they have enough time to bring the mortgage current. Lease Optioners need capital for a down-payment to the owner in hardship, money to bring the property out of hardship, money to clean up and fix the property before finding a Rent-to-Own buyer, and money to make monthly payments to the current homeowner or mortgage company— depending upon the deal structure—until they can get a buyer under contract. After taking control of the home from the current owner, they find a buyer who doesn't yet have the money saved or the credit to purchase a home. The buyer then moves into the home and agrees to purchase it in 3-5 years for the value of the home as predicted after the 3-5 years by the investor. Lease Options provide a short-term monthly gain with 3-5 year payoff when the buyers close on the property. Ownership of the property doesn't change hands until the buyer purchases the property in 3-5 years. Since the Lease Optioner never takes ownership of the property, they don't have to pay any capital gains tax. Their income is made from both the monthly payments, usually $150-$200 per property, and from the difference between what they agree to pay the original owner and what the buyer agrees to pay after the 3-5 years, usually $15,000-$20,000 per property.

Rehabbers are also known as Flippers and Redevelopers. Experienced Rehabbers purchase properties that need repairs, updates, light remodeling, extensive work—including full gut jobs—and aren't afraid to tackle massive water and fire damage. Rehabbers own the properties they work with. They hire experienced contractors or do the repair and/or remodeling work themselves. They have to fund the repairs themselves or make monthly, interest-only payments to a Lender, if they borrowed capital. The average repair cost on most rehab properties is $30-$35 per square foot. Rehabbers also have to pay closing costs, all utilities, and property taxes. Hard Money Lenders are a specific type of Lender that work mostly with Rehabbers. They lend, not based on the present condition of the home, but based on its ARV (After Repair Value), and will sometimes also fund construction budgets. They also charge higher than normal interest rates because their risks are greater than normal lenders. Their rates vary between 9.5% and 16%, based on the deal and, potentially, the credit of the company to whom they are lending. After the home has been returned to a "like new" condition, they sell the home to retail buyers. Rehabbers expect profits of $45,000-$60,000 per home for SFR houses, $20,000-$25,000 per unit for 1-4 unit properties, and $10,000-$15,000 per unit for multi-family properties.

Developers work on large projects like Condo conversions, commercial property conversions, new housing developments, mobile home parks, etc. They work with contractors, and often are contractors. Much of what they purchase is vacant land that doesn't have utility connections installed. Traditional lenders won't fund most development projects because they don't have value until something is developed and most hard money lenders can't work with them because they tend to CAP at $1,000,000 per project. This means that Developers need lots of capital upfront and a pool of real estate lenders for a single project or they need tons of capital to fund the entire project themselves. On the flip side, it typically costs them $85,000 to build a SFR house that they can sell for $225,000-$250,000. In a new housing development, they will build 10-20 homes, sell them, and then use the funds to build between 100-200 homes at $145,000-$165,000 per home in revenue. 100 homes in a new housing development would generate at least $12,000,000 in profit. A Developer's project requires a year or two to complete, lots of due diligence, and a significant investment of time per house.

Lenders have some options. They can work through a company that performs deal due diligence and finds deals for them, through an investment fund—if they are a SEC Certified Investor—and/or directly as a Private Money Lender. Their greatest risk and return is to operate as a Private Money Lender. If the Lender originally started as a Rehabber, operating as a Private Money Lender is your best option. As a former Rehabber, you have the experience and knowledge to evaluate a good deal and determine the best terms. If you have little to no Rehabbing experience and the Rehabbing portion of this book series hasn't been released yet or you don't want to buy it, then I would recommend working through a company that operates as a Hard Money Lending company and doesn't require an SEC Certification. This option offers the lowest ROI and has the second lowest risk. If you have the funds and the ability to become an SEC Certified Investor or are already Certified, the best option is to find a real estate investment fund and lend with them. One of the best around is Gold Coast Capital. Private Money Lenders expect a

10%-12% ROI, Hard Money Lending Investors expect a 6%-7% ROI, and SEC Certified Investors with a good real estate investment fund expect an 8%-10% ROI.

Turn-Key Buyers can purchase homes through a Flip-to-Rent Property Management Company—completely done for you—including property management, or work with a Flip-to-Rent Rehabber to purchase rental properties and find their own property managers. Finding a property management company takes some trial and error and a time investment for due diligence and interviews. Using Flip-to-Rent Property Management Companies will save you time and errors. You should still interview the references of any company and make sure that they will work for you and what you want. Turn-Key Buyers can take advantage of portfolio lenders to maximize their funds and each entity can carry up to 10 conventional mortgages. This allows any knowledgeable or experienced Turn-Key Buyer to leverage their capital to the fullest extent. For SFR and 1-4 unit properties, Turn-Key Buyers should expect $350-$400 profit per unit per month. Multi-unit complexes—10-20 units tend to work best—Turn-Key Buyers should expect $250-$300 per unit per month. With a good property management company, the Turn-

<u>Key Buyer</u> makes the purchase and sits back and collects a paycheck each month.

<u>Bird Dogs</u>, <u>Wholesalers</u>, <u>Lease Optioners</u>, <u>Rehabbers</u>, and <u>Lenders</u> all need to understand the basics of a deal. **There are three basic components to a deal: the property's <u>ARV</u>, the Purchase Price, and the Repair Cost.** In order to calculate these three elements, you need to learn your market, which you can do by capitalizing on the resources available to you. First, you should find a new housing development in the areas where you want to work and note their color themes. Which sells better—cool neutrals or warm? Are open floor plans popular? Stainless steel appliances, white, or black? Over-the-range microwaves, range hoods, island kitchens, wine cabinets, etc.—make a note of any similarities across the majority of model homes. Photograph the home as you walk through it. Stand at cross corners of each room so that you get good photos and an idea of the layout. You are going to look at lots of houses during your time as a real estate investor and you need to be able to remember what houses look like. Using Google Drive, as a free option, or another cloud storage option, save the photos as model homes with the price so that you have a comparison in the future. Getting an

idea of the price of new homes in your area will allow you calculate the price per square foot by dividing the purchase price by the total square footage of the living space of the home.

Using a site like Trulia, Zillow, or Realtor allows you to review the neighborhoods within a given area and review stats such as listing price, sales price, the sale price per square foot, rental prices, crime risks, reported crime incidents, school ratings, district lines, real estate demographics, and commute times. These stats will confirm or formulate an opinion on the viability of a given neighborhood, zip code, area, or city. Once you have an idea of the price per square foot of the better neighborhoods—based on the number of bedrooms, bathrooms, and square footage—you can calculate a starting ARV and grasp which combination of bedroom, bathrooms, and square footage is the sweet spot. In my area, the sweet spot is 3-bedroom, 2-bath homes that are between 1,750 and 2,200 square feet. Our goal is a quick evaluation; use Trulia, Zillow, or Realtor to get the price per square foot of the area where the deal property is located and determine if the area passes as a good neighborhood, based on the stats. Remember that the average repair price per square foot is $30-

$35, so subtract the $35 repair price per square foot from the average sale price per square foot. **Do not offer this amount. This is your cost and does not include any expenses. It will not generate any profit.** Instead, subtract 10% to cover the purchase and sale costs and 1% per month for the estimated number of months based on the contractor's bids. If contractor bids weren't included, then the rule of thumb is one week for every $4,000-$5,000 with professional contractors and one week for every $1,000-$1,500 with a sweat equity investor. Now you need to calculate profit. For new Rehabbers—0-5 completed rehabs—the rule is 20%, or $20,000 minimum. For experienced Rehabbers— more than 5 completed rehabs but not yet doing more than 3 projects at the same time—the rule is 20%, or $30,000 minimum. With Master Rehabbers—more than 3 rehabs at the same time and more than 16 rehabs per year—the rule is 25%, or $45,000, minimum.

To calculate a deal, use the ARV price per square foot minus $30-$35 repair price per square foot, minus 10% for purchase and sale fees, minus 1% per month for expenses, like utilities, and then multiply the remaining price per square foot by the total square feet of the property discussed in the deal. **This number is a snapshot and is used it to calculate the percentage and profit deductions. A good deal means that the purchase price listed in the deal is at least 20% less than your calculated number.** For example: Let's say the deal is for a rehab project for a 1,500 square foot house with 3 bedrooms and 2 bathrooms. Start with the 10%, or $202,500 x 0.1 = $20,250. The average price per square foot for the area where the property is located is $135. So, using the information provided, the estimated repairs are $35 x 1,500 = $52,500 with the repairs estimated at approximately 11 weeks (because $52,500/$5,000 = 10.5 weeks). So, $135 (average price per square feet for the area) - $35 (average estimated repair price per square foot) = $100. Now, $100 x 1,500 (total square footage for the example deals house) = $150,000. So, $150,000 x 0.01 = $1500, and multiplying that by 3 months (11 weeks) = $4,500. Profits are then $150,000 - ($4,500, for expenses, + $20,250, buying and selling fees) = $125,250. Using the 20% and 25% rule gives you $125,250 x 0.20 = $25,050 and $125,250 x 0.25 = $31,312.50. These profit calculations tells us that the offer price for newer Rehabbers should be $105,250 or less, $95,250 for experienced Rehabbers or lower, and $80,250, maximum, for Master Rehabbers.

Remember, this is a rule of thumb. Experienced and Master Rehabbers will probably have lower repair costs per square foot than newer Rehabbers, so you should definitely look over the estimated repair cost included with the deal. Also remember that the goal is an overall assessment to make a determination to look closer at the deal or pass. Therefore, if the deal numbers are close to your calculations (within 10% either up or down), the deal is worth looking at more closely.

Let's practice. Mary is a new Rehabber and is looking for funding for the property she has under contract. Her deal is for a 4-bedroom, 2-bath house of 2,819 square feet. The ARV price per square foot for the area in which this house is located is $185, and her offer price is $275,000. Mary is planning on doing the work herself to save some money, since she is just starting out. What would you say to Mary? If you told Mary that you wouldn't fund her deal because she wouldn't make enough to be profitable, than give yourself a pat on the back. Better yet, if you told Mary that you wanted to fund her deal, if she agreed to use contractors, and you wanted a full deal package, give yourself a gold star! Since the home is 2819 square feet, the estimated repair cost is $98,665 (2819 x

$35/square foot). A professional contractor would take approximately 5 months, ($98,665/$5,000 = 19.733 weeks). While Mary performing the repairs herself, as a <u>sweat equity</u> buyer, it would take approximately 1 year and 5 months ($98,665/$1,500 = 65.77666 weeks). The difference between Mary completing the work herself and hiring contractors is about 11 months and $44,929.77, meaning the difference between a profitable deal and a flop.

READY?

The key takeaways from this chapter are:

- Words underlined are listed and defined in the Glossary section of this chapter
- Don't waste time and effort reinventing the wheel
  - o Remember to get your basket before you go and pick fruit
- The order and ratio of risk to reward for real estate property
  - o Entry and median SFR homes
  - o Mobile homes, Condos, Townhomes, High-End SFR homes
  - o Multi-Units
  - o Commercial
  - o Land
- Know where you should start, based on your availability of time and money, in the real estate investor levels
  - o Bird Dog
  - o Wholesales
  - o Rehabs/Lease Options
  - o Developments
  - o Lenders
  - o Turn-Key Investors
- Understand, at least in general, each level of real estate investing and

have a basic understanding of what is required at each level

- Understand how to evaluate a market, neighborhood, zip code, area or city via websites like Trulia, Zillow or Realtor.com
- Know the three elements of a real estate deal
  - ○ ARV (After Repair Value)
  - ○ Estimated Repair Costs
  - ○ Purchase Price
- Have a good grasp of how to distinguish a good real estate deal from a bad one for the purposes of Bird Dogging, Wholesaling, and/or Lending
- Have a reasonable expectation of profits for all levels of real estate investing

AIM.

In order to reach your full potential, knowledge is critical! The AIM section will help you frame your thoughts and ideas, to capture your mindset, and stimulate and focus your thoughts to take action!

1. Every job you ever had, you learned how to do after you were hired
   - o This book series is your employee manual and new employee orientation
2. Think about your current commitments
   - o How can you reorganize your schedule to maximize your available time?
   - o How much time can you and are you willing to commit to building your Lifestyle by Design?
   - o How much money do you have to invest in yourself as a real estate investor?
   - o Do you have a retirement account and is that retirement account earning you 10%+ annually in profit?

3. What level of real estate investing are you going to start at?
4. What are the profits you can expect from your starting level?
5. What are good neighborhoods and/or areas where you currently live?

FIRE!

TAKE ACTION! Without action, nothing will change. You will not grow or develop, goals will fail, dreams with wither, wealth will remain out of reach, and you won't be able to achieve your Lifestyle by Design. In fact, without action, you will NEVER be able to live your Life by Design.

Get your notebook or journal you used in the previous chapter.

1. Write down a summary of your current schedule on a weekly basis.
2. How much time can you commit to building wealth by working on a level of real estate investing?
3. Write down a new schedule of your week, blocking out the specific time that you are committing to real estate investing.
4. How much working capital do you have? Write it down.
5. Do you currently have a consistent active and investment income? Are you ready to become a Turn-Key Investor?
6. If not, now that you have a schedule with the amount of time you have available on a weekly basis and the amount of working capital you have

available, what level of real estate investor can you start at? Write it down.

7. Return to and read that level's section again. Commit to be involved in that level's description. Write down that level's focus and any other notes on that level's section.

8. Given the profits described in your level and the time and working capital need for the next level, how many times will you have to successfully complete a transaction at your level to reach the next level?

9. Since networking is a large part of so many of the levels, visit http://nationalreia.org/find-a-reia/ and find a local REIA (Real Estate Investor Association) meeting and sign up to attend the next meeting as a guest for free. Write down the date, time, and location, then make a commitment to attend the meeting.

10. When you attend the meeting, let the other investors know that you are new to real estate investing and are starting out at whatever level is your starting level. Make sure you collect business cards and the level each person is operating at currently.

11. Write down a list of all of the better neighborhoods in your area and

navigate to http://www.trulia.com and find the Average Sale Price and Average Sale Price per square foot for homes in those neighborhoods and write them down.

12. With your average sale price per square foot for each neighborhood written down, search homes currently listed for sale in each of the neighborhoods. Search for motivated sellers, handyman specials, pre-foreclosures, distressed, needs work, needs TLC, etc., until you find at least one property for each neighborhood that is currently listed below the average sale price per square foot for the area and write down the square footage, listing price, and the address for each of the properties.

13. Using the snapshot formula to evaluate a good deal, determine if any of the homes you found are good deals and worth a closer look. This is excellent practice!

Now, take a break before you move on to the Afterword, catch your mental breath, and **CELEBRATE** that you took action! **I really, really mean it! Stop and CELEBRATE!**

Iresh Parker

Glossary

1. ***1031 Exchange:*** Tax Code that allows an investor to sell a property to reinvest the proceeds in a new property and to defer all capital gain taxes.

2. ***ARV = After Repair Value***: This is the amount that an investor can expect for a property after the repairs, updates, and redevelopment processes are completed.

3. ***Abatements:*** This is the process whereby a municipality places a lien on a property for the cost of stopping it from being a Nuisance and then forecloses on the property for the dollar amount of the lien. Abatements are a sign of a distressed owner. In some Super-Lien States, the municipality's lien overrules the mortgage.

4. ***Assign/Assignment Contracts:*** This is when you use the assignment clause in a contract to give the rights/privileges of that contract to another person or entity.

5. ***Beneficial Interest:*** This is an entity's amount of benefit in a Trust. A Beneficiary with 10% interest in a Trust is entitled to 10% of the asset(s) in a Trust. Beneficial interest can be sold to another entity either in whole or in part.

6. ***Bird Dogs:*** People who hunt down leads/referrals for another party.

7. ***Buy and Hold:*** A term used to describe an investor that purchases property with the intent of holding onto it rather than selling it.

8. ***Capital Gains:*** Profit from the sale of property or an investment.

9. ***Closing Costs:*** The costs associated with the purchase and/or sale of real estate, often including, but not limited to, things such as the Buyer warranty, the title insurance policy, loan origination fees, appraisal fees, title searches, surveys, taxes, deed-recording fees, homeowner's insurance, and credit report costs.

10. ***Commercial Property:*** Property that is used exclusively for business

purposes and is typically leased out to provide workspace rather than living space. It can also include multi-family property of more than 4 units.

11. *Condos:* Short for condominiums. A condo (condominium) is a private residence owned by an individual in a building or community with multiple units. For real estate investing, condos refers to the larger building or community and not the individual units.

12. *Deal Package:* A packet that Investors send to Lenders when looking for funding. It includes a detailed ARV with 3-5 comps (comparisons); information on the area of the subject property; a current appraisal, such as a BPO (broker price opinion) or CMA (comparative market analysis); a detailed Repair Estimate or 3 contractor bid estimates; a Scope of Work; and photos of the subject property and examples of previously completed, profitable projects (usually a cover page flowed by one page of information on the previous

deal's numbers, one page of before photos and one page of after photos).

13. *Developments/Developers:* A real estate developer is someone who performs development projects, also known as developments. A development is a real estate project that builds, increases, or improves on a current piece of real estate— either land or buildings (also called improvements).

14. *Earnest Money Deposit:* This is a deposit of money made to a seller that represents a buyer's good faith to buy the seller's property. Earnest money is delivered when the purchase contract, option to purchase contract, or sales contract agreement is signed, or money that is given when **the** *offer* *is* *presented.*

15. *Finder's Fee:* This is a preset fee paid by one entity to another entity for bringing it information about a financial investor, a potential new employee, buyers, sellers, or any

relationship which will materially benefit it.

16. *Flip-to-Rent:* This is a term used to describe a Rehab/Flip/Redevelopment project that purchases real estate property with the intention of renting it out after it is completed.

17. *Flippers/Rehabbers/Redevelopers*: An investor who purchases real estate at a discount price and improves the property. Usually they sell the property; however, they may also hold the property to rent it out instead of selling it

18. *Foreclosure:* The judicial act of taking possession of real estate for a number of reasons including a mortgage default, a property tax payment default, an HOA fee default, etc.

19. *Gut Jobs:* This is a rehab project that requires demolition of the home/building down to the stubs, and sometimes 2 of the 4 walls, framing the structure of the house.

20. *Hard Money Lender:* This is a company that specializes in providing hard money loans. Hard money loans are a type of short-term loan financing which is asset-based, allowing a borrower to receive funds secured by real property. They typically have a much shorter duration than conventional loans.

21. *Lender:* This is an entity that provides loans of money to (in this case) real estate investors.

22. *Listing Price:* This is the asking price for a piece of real estate when it is listed. For FSBO (For Sale By Owner) properties, it is the asking price.

23. *Mobile Homes:* These are large trailers or transportable, prefabricated structures that are situated in place and used as permanent living accommodations. They are different than both modular homes and manufactured homes.

24. *Multi-Family:* This is a building or zoning code that is designed or designated as intended to hold more than a single family. This can include

a single family home with a mother-in-law suite or a small apartment over the garage.

25. ***Multi-Unit:*** This is a building(s) that holds more than one individual home. This does not include a single family home with a mother-in-law suite or an apartment over the garage. The smallest form of multi-unit is a duplex.

26. ***Option/Option to Purchase:*** This is representative of an exclusive right to do something. In the case of an option to purchase, it means that the holder of the contract has the exclusive right to purchase a property for the specified length of time.

27. ***Pre-Foreclosures:*** These are part of the foreclosure process where the owner is in default but the home has not been given a foreclosure sale date or the foreclosure sale date has not passed yet.

28. ***Private Money Lender:*** This is a relationship-based lender that loans money to fund (in this case) real

estate transactions. These loans are usually secured by real property

29. **Probates:** As it refers to real estate investing is a property that the court is selling because someone passed away

30. **Property Managers/Property Management Company:** Is a company that is responsible for the operation, control and oversight of a piece of real estate in trust and/or for the benefit of another individual or entity.

31. **Portfolio Lender:** For real estate investors, a portfolio lender is a lender that lends to investors to purchase a portfolio of real estate. This is different from a traditional portfolio lender that has to do with whether or not a lender sells their notes or keeps them in house.

32. **Real Estate Investment Fund:** This can be either a real estate fund or a real estate investment Trust. A real estate fund is a type of mutual fund that primarily focuses on investing in securities offered by public real estate companies. A real estate

investment Trust is also a pool of funds, but it invests directly in income-producing properties and can be traded like stocks or bonds.

33. *Real Estate Investors:* In order to be a real estate investor, **you have to write offers!**

34. *Lease Option:* As it applies to investors, this is a contract between the investor and a tenant which specifies that, at the end of a pre-arranged period of time, the tenant will have the option to purchase the property they leased at the designated price.

35. *Rent-to-Own:* This is a term used to describe the Lease Option process.

36. *ROI = Return On Investment*: This is calculated as a percentage of an investor's total cash contribution divided by total profit. An investor who spent $10,000 of their own money to make $30,000 would have an ROI of 33.33%.

37. *SFR = Single Family Residence:* This is a standard, stick-built home.

38. *Sales Price:* This is the price that a piece of real estate actually sells for after the negotiations.

39. *SEC = U.S. Securities and Exchange Commission:* This is a Federal, independent agency of the government. Their main responsibility is enforcing securities laws and regulating the securities industry. The SEC was created by the Securities Exchange Act of 1934 in the wake of the Great Depression in order to protect investors.

40. *SEC Certified Investor:* This is an investor—either an individual or entity—who is allowed to deal in securities that are not registered with the financial authorities. They have to satisfy one or more specific requirements with regards to income, net worth, asset size, governance status, or professional experience. If you have a net worth in excess of $1,000,000, made $200,000/year for the last two years and have an expectation of making $200,000 or more in the current year or have a Trust with assets in excess of $5,000,000 speak with an attorney

who specializes in working with the SEC about becoming an accredited investor.

41. *Short Sales:* A short sale is when a home is sold for less that the outstanding debt on the home.

42. *Sweat Equity:* As it applies to real estate investing, is an owner who does the property improvements that increase the property's value themselves.

43. *Tax Lien:* This is a lien that is placed on real estate for unpaid taxes, income taxes, property taxes, or any other kind of taxes.

44. *Townhomes:* A townhome is where several units are conjoined and the buildings and units are owned by individuals while the property and community buildings are owned by the owner of real estate. These are similar to condos (except that condo owners own the individual units but not the building that the condo units are inside of). For real estate investment purposes, townhomes refer to the collection of conjoined buildings and not the individual units.

45. *Turn-Key Buyers:* These are investors who purchase turn-key properties.

46. *Turn-Key Properties*: These are homes, apartments, and/or apartment buildings that have been fully renovated, remodeled, and have a leased tenant in place. They are designed to limit the amount of time and effort on the part of the investor.

47. *Under Contract:* This refers to real estate that has some kind of signed contract, either a purchase-and-sale agreement or an option-to-purchase agreement.

48. *Underwater:* This refers to a piece of real estate that is worth less than the debt owed on it.

49. *Vacant Land:* As it pertains to real estate, is land that has no improvements, which include living space.

50. *Wholesale:* In real estate investing, this is a process where an individual or entity secures a piece of real estate with either a signed purchase-and-sale agreement or an option-to-

purchase agreement and markets the option, contract, or property to other real estate investors.

Afterword: Building a Team of Experts

Leveraging expertise is a powerful and necessary process of success and a large part of building long-lasting, win-win relationships. Supercharging your success and increasing the speed of achieving it is easier when you have experts to assist you. We have already talked about CPAs/accountants and attorneys. We also discussed building relationships with other investors. Bird Dogs, Wholesalers, Rehabbers, Developers, Lenders and Turn-Key Buyers are all highlighted investors, but don't miss property managers, contractors, and Buy and Hold investors. But who else?

One of the best professionals for investors to build relationships with is Real Estate Agents or Brokers. Many real estate investors will tell you to not work with Real Estate Brokers because their commissions cut into your profits. They will say that Real Estate Agents are your competition. **There is no competition**. Working together creates win-win situations, creating *more* for everyone! That's not competition! A very limited view sees a Real Estate Broker's commission as taking away from an investor's bottom line. However, 85% of all real estate sales in the United States take place from the MLS (Multiple Listing System), which is a database comprised of real estate property listed by Licensed Real Estate Principles, Brokers and Agents. Experienced, professional investors knows that paying a 3%-6% commission to a good Real Estate Broker who brings you 5-7 property deals a month is worth it because you are making more together, creating a win-win.

You are also leveraging their expertise. Real Estate Agents look at houses all of the time. They spend their days walking through houses, marketing to owners, and networking within the real estate industry. A good Real Estate Broker that you have developed a relationship with will walk through a house and take pictures for you to give you an idea of estimated repairs. They will adjust their commissions if they can represent both sides of a transaction—when you buy the property and when you sell it—and they will Bird Dog for you for free. They also have their own real estate team in place. You can leverage through them as well. They include title company agents, mortgage brokers, and maybe even contractors. They are a great place to start building your team!

Additionally, there are Agents that are REO—real estate owned (property that has been foreclosed on by a bank and the bank now owns)—agents who list properties for banks and are an excellent source for distressed properties. Building a relationship with a good REO broker gets you access to shadow inventory—REO properties that aren't listed yet but will be soon—allowing you to get your offers in before anyone else. This is very beneficial since most good deals are under contract within 48 hours of being listed.

You will also need a few good contractors on your team. You are looking for contractors in good standing with your state's contractor's board and a good rating with the Better Business Bureau. You want a General Contractor who does most of their own work and only subcontracts specialties to help save you money. You also want your contractor to have several years of experience. In addition to a General Contractor, you will also need to form relationships with Electricians, Plumbers, and HVAC contractors. Eventually, you will also need to work with architects and engineers. A good General Contractor, just like a good Real Estate Broker, will typically have a team in place that includes most of these specialty contractors.

Other than attending your local REIA meeting, what else could you do to start networking and developing relationships with these individuals? Write down 5 ideas in your journal and commit to 3 of the actions.

Next Steps: Looking for More

We have arrived at the end the first step in our journey together! Take some time and celebrate! When you are done, visit me on the Inspirational Business Website at www.inspirationalbusiness.us where you can:

- Click "Access Free" and enter your name and email address to sign-up for the newsletter and get your free goals worksheet

- Review all of the supplemental workbooks, calculators and worksheets available for Step 1 to help accelerate your success

- Pre-Order Step #2: Deal or No Deal

- Review the Next Steps training options and videos to catapult your wealth building

- Peruse designing wellness products

- Visit our YouTube channel, Profit Avalanche, and subscribe for free to be updated with weekly videos

- Visit the Profit Avalanche website at www.profitavalanche.site to

complete a free assessment to guide
you to making fast money online

ABOUT THE AUTHOR

Before becoming a successful real estate investor, Iresh was a Loss Mitigation Specialist, either providing solutions to avoid foreclosure via a loan repayment plan, a loan modification, or a deed in lieu of foreclosure. Seeing borrower after borrow progress through the loss mitigation process and lose their homes, Iresh became frustrated, wanting to help, and was sanctioned at work for providing real suggestions and solutions to borrowers. Iresh decided to get out of the game of helping banks make more money, destroying the middle class in this country and making a lie of the American dream.

Understanding the need for education, Iresh built real estate expertise over time and after a rocky start, became a successful real estate investor. Iresh has been an active and successful investor for more than 11 years, continuing to make money and build wealth through both the real estate market crash in 2008 and the second downturn in 2010. In 2014, Iresh started getting tons of requests from other real estate investors, wanting to learn. They were coming out of the woodwork from all over the country and wanted to pay Iresh for a proper real estate education. In 2015, Iresh became a mentor and began training active investors. In an effort to create a better future, started working with their children. From these trainings and education came the inception of the *Lifestyle by Design* series and the 8-Step Guide began.

2018 brought an additional challenge when Iresh's inbox and voicemail were flooded with a new kind of request, not from active real investors, as previously noted, but from brand new people wanting to improve their lives by becoming real estate investors and reaching out for education and mentorship. With experienced, active investors, Iresh ran the education program with 6-8 investors and one additional guest, for a total of 12-16 people in a 6-month training certification program. Mentorship, of course, was for life. If Iresh was going to start working with squeaky new investors, then the program would have to be much smaller and should be divided. Iresh wanted to help as many people as possible and so suggested that the new real estate investors find and participate in a real estate investing educational program. Unfortunately, the suggestion brought even more contact because there were no cost-effective, good educational programs out there that provided mentor level support.

Determined to find a good real estate investment educational program for less than $5,000, Iresh began studying the world of investor education and found the feedback 100% accurate. The good programs offered 6 months of coaching and mentorship and were running at $10,000 and above. The best programs charged in excess of $25,000, and offered 12 months of coaching and mentorship. What was a new real estate investor to do? Most of the interested, potential students didn't have the money to pay $10,000-$25,000 in educational costs, plus have additional money to set up their business and build their team—not to mention market for deals. The space in the author's office would not hold the thousands of people reaching out daily, either! Suddenly, like a lighting strike from above, Iresh found the

Self-Publishing School and created an answer.

Now Iresh can reach hundreds of thousands of people for a small investment via the *Lifestyle by Design* series and the 8 Steps books. Iresh can use the books to sift the chaff and find the truly dedicated and coachable action-takers, to balance the wealth equation, and to help the greatest number of individuals and their families.

Here is my giving back.

If you really want a change and are committed to taking action to create a positive change in your mind, yourself, and your life, then please follow the Ready, Aim, Fire sections through all of the Next Steps and Iresh will help you with the stepping stones to your future and your dreams!

Can You Help?

Thank you for reading my book!

I really appreciate feedback, and want to hear what you have to say.

Please leave me an honest review on Amazon or on Inspirational Business, wherever you purchased it, letting me know what you thought of the book.

I will use your input to make the next books in *Lifestyle by Design: An 8-Step Guide to Building Wealth* series even better!

Thanks so much!

~Iresh

A Bonus for You

Discover the EXACT 3-step blueprint you need to become a bestselling author in 3 months.

Self-Publishing School helped me, and now I want them to help you with this FREE WEBINAR! Even if you're busy, bad at writing, or don't know where to start, you CAN write a bestseller and build your best life.

With tools and experience across a variety of niches and professions, Self-Publishing School is the only resource you need to take your book to the finish line!